EDUCATION AND THE INDIVIDUAL

Unwin Education Books

Series Editor: Ivor Morrish, BD, BA, Dip.Ed (London), BA (Bristol)

Education and the Individual

BRENDA COHEN
Lecturer in Philosophy, University of Surrey

London
GEORGE ALLEN & UNWIN
Boston   Sydney

First published in 1981

GEORGE ALLEN & UNWIN LTD
40 Museum Street, London WC1A 1LU

© George Allen & Unwin (Publishers) Ltd 1981

ISBN 0-04-370108-6
     0-04-370109-4 Pbk

Set in 10 on 11 point Times by The Drawing Room, Ashford
and Printed in Great Britain
by Billing & Sons Ltd Guildford, London and Worcester

Contents

If the State does for the individual what he ought to do for himself what will be the effect on character, initiative, enterprise?

(H. Hobhouse, *Liberalism)*

The great lesson which the individualist philosophy teaches us . . . is that, while it may not be difficult to destroy the spontaneous formations which are the indispensable bases of a free civilization, it may be beyond our power deliberately to reconstruct such a civilization once these foundations are destroyed.

(F. A. Hayek, *Individualism and Economic Order*)

Preface

This is not a book against equality, but for freedom. Nor is it for anarchy against order, but rather for choice against educational coercion. Although there is a tendency to make educational debate match the lines of political parties, this is not a book from the political right against the political left but rather from a liberal standpoint as opposed to the standpoint of totalitarianism. This is a distinction which cuts across the left/right categorisation of recent educational controversy. Indeed, an integral part of the case that is presented here is that these hardening political demarcations have obscured the essential principles on which, with much wider application than any particular modern society, educational arrangements should be based.

Education is an area where misplaced convictions can do a maximum of harm to society, and it seems to me that for the best and most idealistic of reasons many people involved with the educational process have been persuaded to endorse a facile sociological viewpoint which conditions them to see students in schools solely as representatives of a class and not as individuals. They then seek causal explanations of their behaviour and performance along lines which ignore the essential freedom of each individual to determine his own path and strategy through life. Imperfect correlations are built into iron laws. A deterministic and egalitarian philosophy is presented and accepted as scientific truth. My purpose has been to counter this trend and to reassert the importance of the individual and the family in the area of education.

I should like to thank Professor D. J. O'Connor of Exeter University for reading a draft of this book and for making detailed comments which encouraged me to clarify what was obscure and think again about what was doubtful. The overall viewpoint, however, is a personal one which I leave it to the reader to judge in the light of his own convictions and experience.

I should like to thank the editor of the *Journal of Philosophy of Education,* R. S. Peters, for permission to use my article 'Equality, freedom and independent schools', *Journal of Philosophy of Education,* vol. 12, 1978, as the basis for Chapter 3.

Chapter 1

Introduction

For a child to be taken from the care of his parents and the company of his brothers and sisters and placed in institutional care when no fault or problem has been found with the child himself and when the *begs* parents concerned have provided for him all the expected amenities of *the* life is something which demands explanation. It is a situation, though, *question* which has occurred from time to time in recent years even in the liberal democratic context of Britain. Circumstances have varied from case to case, but in general the element in the situation which has produced this result has been a disagreement between parents and state over the form which their children's education should take. In the eyes of those professionally responsible the fact that the parents are failing to provide education for their child is the justification for their intervention, however drastic; in the eyes of the parents the provision by the state of only a type of education to which they object is a justification for their failure to comply with the education authority's demands.

And yet the principle that education should be compulsory is not usually seen as a violation of parental rights, but rather as a guarantee of the rights of the child. The conflict arises when parents look to the state as the natural supplier of the commodity of education; and as alternatives diminish, the strains increase, so that ultimately the phrase 'alternative schooling' becomes a slogan not merely of the traditional supporters of private non-state education, but also of alienated individuals in more financially straitened sections of society. For some, 'free schools' have provided a solution; for others hard-bought financial sacrifice has enabled a wider freedom of choice; but in other cases the sacrifice has been on the part of the child caught between the requirements of the state and the assertion of parental rights.

The resolution of this conflict is not merely a matter in which the happiness of a small and in many ways exceptional group of children is at issue. Nor is it only a matter of assessing the rival claims of comprehensive and selective schools, independent and state-funded schools, or specialised and general education. The problem is more fundamental than this. The structure of education for any one generation of children has a strong determining influence on the shape and structure of the future society which their expectation and beliefs will create. In a more literal sense than is usually noticed, today's schools are tomorrow's society. It would not be surprising, then, if the principles and structures of education in a liberal society were to diverge very considerably from those of a totalitarian society; nor if the continued existence of a liberal society were to turn out to depend very closely on the ability of educators in a liberal society to identify, understand and then work to preserve these distinguishing features. It is clear, then, that political and social principles are closely involved with what might be termed questions of educational ideology, and in particular with the question of the balance of power and influence as between the state as an organisation on the one hand, and the individual on the other.

The discussion which follows is a discussion of this balance; an examination of the ideologies involved in differing positions; and an investigation of the implications of the individual's surrender of the control of education to the state.

Before considering the more fundamental question, however, it will be necessary to examine the position of those who advocate the limitation of parental choice and the extension of state control. These include first of all those whose concern is to accomplish this within the state system itself; and then secondly those who look beyond the limits of the state system and advocate banning or limiting educational activities altogether outside its framework. This will lead to consideration of the rival claims of children and parents, in so far as the state's intervention may be justified as protecting the former against the latter. Only when these matters have been considered will it be possible to turn to the central task of weighing the claims of the individual and state in respect of education.

Chapter 2

Selective Education and the Goal of Equality

State financing of education is consistent with a high degree of individual or at least local control of the nature and form of education. A system in which parents were issued with vouchers for educational services cashable at institutions of their choice, or payable to private tutors, could still be defined as state provision, although state control would be minimal. Between such a system and a system of centralised direction and inspection lies a whole continuum of possibilities. Which possibility is chosen by a society will depend on the answers tacitly assumed by that society to a number of questions. Is education the business of the state? Or is it essentially a matter for the family? Is the state's responsibility finished when it sees that the family has fulfilled *its* responsibilities? Or is there an educational function which can be fulfilled only on a public rather than a private basis?

For one group of people these questions must be answered decisively in favour of the state. These are people whose position is defined in terms of their attitude to equality. For while many educational aims may be attained by private effort, the goal of equality is inconsistent with anything other than a publicly administered and closely monitored system of control. Both the possibility of some obtaining a better education than the majority, and of others receiving an education which is recognisably worse, must be guarded against if equality is to be achieved. Thus are born the twin policies of positive discrimination on the one hand, to remedy disadvantage, and opposition to selection on the other, to curb advantage.

The case for the first of these policies starts from a moral presumption in favour of diverting resources from those privileged either by natural talent or by social position to those less advantageously placed. As a practical administrative policy this involves the identification and specification of certain types of recognisable disadvantage, race, sex, social class and occasionally geographical region having been particularly singled out for action. But at school and at classroom level, it is a policy which finds its expression in the idea that the able can, on the whole, educate themselves; and that such special assistance as may be obtainable should be devoted to the under-achiever. Indeed, that the ideal being aimed at is one of levelling of performance is appropriately illustrated by the journalistic coining of a new word expressing a theoretically ungrounded new concept, 'over-achiever'. Although sometimes argued for in terms of the goal of equality of opportunity, the test of success of such policies tends to be equality of outcome, so that it is the latter rather than the former goal which is most closely identified with positive discrimination.

The second policy is based at least partly on an assumption of the essential injustice or unfairness of advantage. Equality and justice, however, are very different goals. For justice is essentially bound up with the recognition of relevant difference; the notions of justice and desert are inseparable. This point was most succinctly put by Aristotle when he said that injustice consists as much in treating unequals equally as in treating equals unequally. On this proportionate view, strict egalitarianism can involve the advocacy of injustice. Justice may require the recognition of relevant differences and their differential treatment; equality the elimination of differences by methods of public policy.

The justification for pursuing the goal of equality may be based on considerations of either morality or expediency. In the first case it will be argued that equality is morally desirable in itself, without further justification; in the second case, that it is of benefit to the community in promoting an overall increase in efficiency, wealth and happiness. The former viewpoint, which bases the objection to inequality on intuitive or *a priori* grounds rather than on practical grounds requires that inequality be eliminated at any cost, and a demonstration that the cost is high in material terms will not be decisive. The second ground for egalitarianism, however, produces a more moderate and more commonly held view, according to which inequality is only one amongst a number of evils, and equality only one amongst a number of goods. Where this view is held, the sacrifices of other goods which must be made for the egalitarian cause will be weighed without bias and without any prior judgement in favour of equality.

In the world of education these two forms of egalitarianism are particularly significant in determining attitudes towards such major policy issues as comprehensive or selective education, or the encouragement or discouragement of a private sector of education financed independently of the state. While the second and more moderate form of egalitarianism in recognising other goods than equality leaves educational policy open, or at least dependent on empirical findings, the first and stronger form, particularly when combined with the doctrine of the moral indifference of individual character, is inflexible in ruling out most forms of differential schooling. Specifically, while the second will be influenced by the question of the educational efficiency of social equalisation policies, the first will dismiss this aspect as essentially irrelevant.

The practical case for seeking to redress the balance of nature and of circumstances by a policy of positive discrimination - by supplying more and better education to those at a disadvantage - and for restraining the progress of the advantaged by control of the structure of schools and of classes within schools may, however, be based on considerations of utility. In this case it will be derived from the at first sight extremely persuasive presumption that arrangements should be publicly made which are for the greatest general welfare of the citizens of a state. It is assumed that this requirement is not being met if some of the citizens of that state are conspicuously lacking in educational attainment as compared with others.

The practical and moral case for basic minimum standards is easy to justify, but minimum is a relative concept, and conspicuous high attainment by some will have the effect of constantly inflating the level at which comparisons are made, rather in the way in which improved economic conditions alter the criteria for specifying unacceptable levels of poverty. As a result, continuous improvement at the higher levels will itself adversely affect the possibility of raising the lowest standards to what can be considered acceptable. In absolute terms improvement may be achieved, but the relative position, which forms a more potent psychological yardstick, will continue to worsen. For this reason, a policy of improving the situation of the worst-off, if it is to be recognisably successful, cannot involve even-handed distribution of resources, but must necessarily involve some restraint on the situation of the better-off. Hence a reluctance to allow the existence of what might be termed 'super-schools' in any sense whatever, whether as academically selective schools, privately financed schools, schools for gifted children, or specialist institutions for the musically, artistically or otherwise talented. But if this is a utilitarian argument, it may be countered by the consideration that the fostering of special talent, even genius, *is* in the wider interest of society even if elitist institutions are necessary to achieve this end. Any objection which pays attention to the relative standard of education in a society rather than the absolute, moreover, while psychologically understandable, is essentially based on allowing envy to play a determining part in the organisation of society. If it would be wrong to seek to maximise the happiness of a society by fulfilling its racist aspirations, then it would be equally wrong to pander to straight-forward anti-elitist prejudice.

But this is to shift the argument from grounds of utility - which are arguable, but only on the basis of fact - to grounds of morality, and it is here that genuine philosophical disagreement is to be found. The moderate egalitarian of utilitarian outlook essentially makes the modest claim that equality is a good, if it can be achieved without a net loss of benefit to society as a whole, and he may even be prepared to concede that homogeneity itself could be a distasteful factor reducing the possibilities for happiness in a community. Like Mill, he might admit the importance of variety, eccentricity, distinction in the arts and sciences or in physical performance. But the defender of the more extreme view demands radical change, is not prepared to see things left much as they were before he made his demand for equality, and indeed is prepared to see sacrifices made in its cause. Neither pragmatic nor practical considerations provide the strongest support for the radical egalitarian's position, but rather an intuitive presumption in favour of equality. As with all intuitionist positions, the failure of others to share this valuation is not an appropriate occasion for rational disputation, but rather for persuasion and influence - the placing of matters in a certain light, which may be instrumental in a conversion of attitude. The question arises, then, what kind of considerations might meet this requirement in the case of educational equality?

A passage from John Rawls's *A Theory of Justice* gives some indication of what sort of considerations these might be, but first it is necessary to set Rawls's remarks on education in the context of his wider social theory. In *A Theory of Justice* Rawls is concerned to establish those principles of justice which 'free and rational persons concerned to further their own interests would accept in an initial position of equality as defining the fundamental terms of their association'.[1] The original state of equality referred to here is defined by Rawls as one of ignorance of such factors as the place in society to be occupied by the participants, their social class, status, natural assets and abilities, intelligence, strength and, in addition, their conceptions of good, or special psychological propensities. This postulate is referred to as the 'veil of ignorance' and is designed to secure impartiality of judgement on the part of participants who are taken to be both self-interested and rational. Their concern is to distribute such social goods as rights and liberties, opportunities and power, income and wealth and self-respect. The basic principle arrived at for this distribution is that these goods should be distributed equally unless an unequal distribution is to the advantage of the least favoured, since this is the only principle which guarantees the largest possible share to any individual. Rawls believes that his rational and self-interested participants would allot priority to a principle of liberty, but subject to this he sees the principle just described, which he calls the maximin principle (in fact the rule for choice under uncertainty which specifies that in uncertainty one should choose the course which has the best worst outcome) as most likely to commend itself in the circumstances specified. The manner in which Rawls applies this principle to education is indicated in this brief passage:

> Chances to acquire cultural knowledge and skills should not depend upon one's class position, and so the school system, whether public or private, should be designed to even out class barriers.
>
> While the liberal conception seems clearly preferable to the system of natural liberty, intuitively it still appears defective. For one thing, even if it works to perfection in eliminating the influence of social contingencies, it still permits the distribution of wealth and income to be determined by the natural distribution of abilities and talents. Within the limits allowed by the background arrangements, distributive shares are decided by the outcome of the natural lottery; and this outcome is arbitrary from a moral perspective. There is no more reason to permit the distribution of income and wealth to be settled by the distribution of natural assets than by historical and social fortune. Furthermore, the principle of fair opportunity can be only imperfectly carried out, at least as long as the institution of the family exists. The extent to which natural capacities develop and reach fruition is affected by all kinds of conditions and class attitudes. Even the willingness to make an effort, to try, and so to be deserving in the ordinary sense is itself dependent on happy family and social circumstances.[2]

This statement sums up very well many radical preoccupations and presuppositions within education - the notion of the arbitrariness of the distribution of natural talents, perhaps even including that of a willingness to work hard; the recognition - though challenged by some - that there is a relation between academic success and income and wealth later in life; the recommendation that the school system should be used to even out social class differences; and the drawing back from the brink of the suggestion that ultimately only the elimination of the family could finally and completely overcome these discrepancies in individual life-chances.

Rawls himself, as he makes clear, does not take this ultimate step, and indeed, within the overall framework of the social theory described in *A Theory of Justice,* while equal education features as a prerequisite of a just society, this is only in the sense in which equal education is something that can be achieved by some public provision of education as well as subsidies for private education. Rawls, too, whilst querying the moral relevance of differences of natural endowment and circumstances, does make the assumption that such differences exist, even while insisting that these ought not to count in the distribution of life's prizes. Others, of course, are prepared to pursue these theoretical reflections to less qualified conclusions. Rawls's remarks, however, tend to confuse the question of material rewards for differences in ability and differential effort with the question of the appropriateness of different educational treatment. The reason why educational equality and economic equality become linked in this way in contemporary liberal discussion is no doubt that this discussion takes place within the context of a society which is itself based on the principle of the recognition of merit and the linking of material reward with educational attainment. It has recently been argued that this link is to some extent illusory and that much more depends on chance in a person's material standard of life than on differences of education. However, the widespread assumption that there is such a connection accounts for the position of one who, like Rawls, is essentially willing to justify an entrepreneurial society so long as some of the harsher aspects of competition are eliminated, but would regard equalisation of the starting-point for this competition as a condition of fairness.

In *Anarchy, State and Utopia,* however, Robert Nozick adopts a very different perspective from Rawls. He argues for the justification of only a minimal state - the 'nightwatchman' state of classical liberal theory, limited to the narrow functions of protection against force, theft, fraud and enforcement of contracts. Anything more extensive, he maintains, will violate a person's rights against coercion. This applies in particular both to welfare and paternalistic legislation, areas which are central to education. Nozick argues against Rawls's principle of fairness and in favour of historical-entitlement principles. Touching briefly and indirectly on the subject of education, he says:

> One indication of the stringency of Rawls' difference principle . . . is its inappropriateness as a governing principle even within a family of individuals who love one another. Should a family devote its resources to maximising the position of its least well off and least talented child, holding back the other children or using resources for their education and development only if they will

follow a policy throughout their lifetime of maximising the position of their least fortunate sibling? Surely not. How then can this even be considered as the appropriate policy for enforcement in the wider society?[3]

These brief remarks give some indication of the underlying differences implicit in the two approaches. For Rawls what is arbitrary includes basic aspects of a person's character, as well as the accidents of birth and social status. For Nozick, these are the raw material of personal identity from which the individual should be left free by others and by government to widen and increase the differentiation between himself and others. For those who sympathise with Rawls's point of view, equality of outcome would be the educational goal which would have most appeal; for those more disposed to the ideals of Nozick, equality of opportunity would provide all that a state might validly seek to supply.

For the educational radical, plainly the moral indifference of initial intellectual and emotional endowment is a primary consideration, and the case for it may be persuasively put, as in this quotation from Hastings Rashdall:

> In most men at least this feeling [of humility] will be strengthened by the recognition that the differences between themselves and their fellows are largely due . . . not to any efforts which begin exclusively with themselves. To use theological language, the good man will ascribe his goodness to 'grace' recognising that his good qualities are due in the first instance to parentage, influence, example, social tradition, education, community, Church and ultimately, if he is a religious man, to God.[4]

But the claim that one should treat character and ability as morally indifferent factors is extremely problematic. The suggestion that one should do so may be based, as in this passage, on the fact that many differences of character can be traced, not to initial innate endowment, but to identifiable social and environmental conditions - factors which are clearly outside the individual's own control. But then his initial endowment is equally outside his own control in this sense, so that from this point of view the causal origins of character, whether genetic or environmental, are strictly irrelevant. In the attempt to search for assignable blame one might imagine an - as yet - science-fiction situation in which genetic engineering reached a stage where pre-natal control of intelligence and character could be guaranteed to a careful and responsible parent. In this case, to give birth to a child who was morally or intellectually limited would be a matter for moral condemnation. If it happened accidentally, as a result of medical incompetence, for example, or from a failure on the part of the government to provide adequate funds for the necessary medical investigations, then society might well be said to have an obligation to compensate such a child for its disadvantages. Outside this science-fiction situation, such a claim is more likely to be made on behalf of certain classes in society, or ethnic minorities, or women, any of whom may be held to be handicapped by their situation.

In considering the strength of the moral position, though, the more fanciful case is the more illuminating. What it reveals is that questions of personal identity and also questions concerning determinism and free will are implicit in the discussion. The former type of question arises when it is asked who is the subject who ought to be compensated for not being the person he might have been? Where a physical handicap is involved, as in the case of the thalidomide tragedy, this is not an incoherent question and it is possible to give a reasonably clear answer. There is a spiritual, emotional and intellectual being whose loss can be determined in the light of a readily agreed physical norm. But where the loss is one affecting personality, and where normality is a controversial matter of judgement, the coherence of the question and the possibility of answering it adequately are both in doubt. This is particularly the case when it is suggested that a person should be compensated for lacking the strength of will to make himself other than he happens to be. Implicit in this position is a suggestion that it may not be someone's fault that he does not want to try to avoid, for example, criminality, or ignorance. But can anything be made of this suggestion of an inner controller of character? A regress of this kind, once started, may be infinite. Rather than embark on it, it is preferable to say simply that a person is the person that he is, as defined by his character, abilities, dispositions, potentialities, and so on.

This is not to deny that to offer education for unfulfilled potential may be both possible and morally required. But to aim at some uniform 'character' for everybody is to make injustifiable deterministic assumptions. To take the variety of human character and endowment, then, as given, and to recognise that individual human choice and action flow from individual character, far from involving acceptance of the determinism implied in Rawls's remarks, is to recognise free will in the only sense that is relevant to the attribution of responsibility. Even if the appraisal of character is held to be a quasi-aesthetic process, it is still the case that people are to be praised or blamed for the traits of personality which they betray in their actions. Character is not, as Rawls suggests, morally indifferent - or at least only in a sense in which *everything* may be said to be morally different. Rawls, however, implies a contrast as do those radicals who share his point of view - that while *character* is as morally indifferent as historical and social fortune, there remains something to which the notion of moral responsibility may be attached. But once the implied contrast is spelled out in this way, it is clear that there can be no other candidate for moral responsibility. Hence it is not wrong to respond differentially to differences of character. In the same way differences of initial intellectual and emotional endowment are not morally insignificant factors and therefore justify differentiated treatment.

This applies where educational 'goods' are in question. It does not, of course, immediately affect the question of material equality, for which it may more plausibly be held that natural assets are morally indifferent. To vary the example suggested by Nozick, a parent may not wish to see his less able child worse fed or worse attired than his most able. If he can send only one to university, however, then both ability and willingness to work may well be considerations he takes into account. But if the link between educational attainment, seen as a product of ability and application on the one hand and material reward on the other, is allowed to become too remote, it has to be recognised that a consequence of this must be a deterioration in the standing of education, and probably, though not inevitably, a corruption of culture. Briefly, it is hard both to claim that intellectual and moral qualities are valuable (in either a moral or an aesthetic sense) and to claim that society should be organised in such a way as to deny them their natural rewards. It is true that only certain kinds of meritocratic society do render these rewards natural, and also true that there have been many societies - those organised on a rigid caste or class basis, for example - where such intellectual and moral qualities have been of no advantage to their possessor; but if we start, as in modern liberal societies we tend to do, from a roughly meritocratic position, strong arguments are needed for an organised retreat through the medium of education in the direction indicated by egalitarians.

These are arguments against a strong egalitarian position - a position which asserts the value of equality even in the face of practical losses to society, such as an increase in poverty and a diminishing of welfare or economic goods. They are arguments which tend to favour a policy of leaving much to the interaction of individuals acting privately, in ways which depend on their personal character and ability, with chance playing a major role in determining actual consequences. They are arguments against a form of egalitarianism which involves, in terms of Rawls's difference principle, a situation in which the position of the worst-off as well as the better-off in society is made even worse than it might have been had equality not been assigned over-riding priority.

It remains to consider, though, what may be said of that moderate form of egalitarianism which limits itself to more modest demands. Like the stronger form it may find its expression in the demand for a common school based on the mutual respect of all members of a community. But it may concede that the value of such an arrangement as an expression of community feeling and cohesiveness depends on the voluntary nature of the association and the existence of alternatives. So presented, the common school will be a particularly acceptable arrangement in the case of young children and of small communities. But a common school need not mean a common, or the same, education. A school attended by all, or nearly all, the children of a particular neighbourhood may still recognise diversity of interest and talent and set itself the goal of fostering those interests and developing those talents; it need not be governed by the unrealistic aim of homogenisation of educational product. If there is a moderate form of egalitarianism which would accept the wide differences in attainment in various areas of knowledge and performance which would inevitably result, then this would be consistent with the trend in the development of educational policy in Britain and other European countries over the past fifty years. So much has a belief in the appropriateness of differential treatment been a presumption of public policy in education that it is easy to overlook the homogeneity of approach, relative only to social class, that characterised schooling before this date. But as long ago as 1926, the Hadow Report included the words: 'Equality is not identity; the educational system should not attempt to press different types of children into an identical mould.'

It was this principle that was enshrined in the well-known phrase from the 1944 Education Act laying down that education should be in accordance with 'age, aptitude and ability'. Some supporters of comprehensive reorganisation saw this reorganisation as the most efficient way of finally securing this good. Others, however, explicitly rejected such a goal in preference for the goal of equalisation. In the memorable phrase of Eric Midwinter, these egalitarians wish to see the goal of equality of opportunity replaced by that of an opportunity of equality. It was an earlier writer, R. H. Tawney, however, who first articulated criticism of the principle of equality of opportunity when he described it as a Tadpole Philosophy; meaning by this that it provides a means of escape for the fortunate few, whilst leaving the majority to eke out a miserable and underprivileged existence in the stagnant pool of a radically inegalitarian society. Nevertheless, Tawney should not be interpreted anachronistically as wholly repudiating the idea of selective and differentiated education, for he added the following remarks of very different implication:

> What a wise parent would desire for his own children, that a nation, is so far as it is wise, must desire for all children. Educational equality consists of securing it for them. It is to be achieved in school, as it is achieved in the home, by recognising that there are diversities of gifts, which require for their development diversities of treatment. Its aim will be to do justice to all, by providing facilities which are at once various in type and equal in quality[5].

This concession to differential treatment is not, though, an endorsement of the meritocratic principle, a principle whose effects were satirised by Michael Young in 'The rise of the meritocracy'. His picture of a society in which the able few exploit the weak majority, shorn of their natural leaders and spokesmen, discredited for many the idea of meritocracy, but the implications of its rejection have not been widely recognised. The right of a society to seek out latent talent - to gear occupations to educational qualifications and educational qualifications to individual ability - is not only an essentially moral claim, but also a matter of practical expediency. A bus conductor whose mathematical skills exceed those of a university mathematics professor is not merely inappropriately positioned from the point of view of his own satisfaction, but represents also a loss to society. The meritocratic principle simply recognises that this situation and its reverse are anomalous; those who would deny it irrationally and immorally accept these anomalies to the detriment of all.

It follows, then, that meritocracy, entailing as it does practical procedures of competition and selection, has a sound basis in both morality and practical utility. And while a meritocratically ordered society may order its schools in a variety of different ways, neither equality of attainment as a goal nor equality of education as a practice is consistent with a meritocratic outcome. Equality of opportunity may be more efficient in achieving such an outcome, but even this principle must be more generously interpreted than has been the case in recent educational debate. In particular it should not be supposed that the principle of equality of opportunity has been betrayed when it has been found not have produced equality of attainment. For the variables affecting educational outcomes include the differences between the human beings involved in the educational process. Differential education and the practice of selection merely acknowledge this fact. Moreover, while the democratic principle of equality might seem to be served by attempts to cancel out such differences, the democratic principle of freedom would not be so served. The enforcement of equality, then, by the imposition of a system of education offering no scope for choice or individual variation does not have the monopoly of moral and rational justification that its proponents claim. This is true whether the enforcement takes the form of positive discrimination on the one hand, or opposition to 'super-schools' on the other. In terms of both morality and rationality, these practical techniques of equalisation are without justification.

NOTES: CHAPTER 2

1 J. Rawls, *A Theory of Justice* (London: Oxford University Press, 1972), p. 11.
2 ibid., pp. 73-4.
3 R. Nozick, *Anarchy, State and Utopia* (Oxford: Blackwell, 1974), p. 167, footnote.
4 Hastings Rashdall, *Theory of Good and Evil,* 2nd edn (London: Oxford University Press, 1924), Vol. I, p. 206, quoted by H. Spiegelberg, 'Defense of human equality', in W. T. Blackstone (ed.), *The Concept of Equality* (Minneapolis, Minn.: Burgess, 1969).
5 R. H. Tawney, *Equality* (London: Allen & Unwin, 1964), p. 146.

Chapter 3

The Issue of Independent Schools

In the preceding chapter it was argued that individual differences in both ability and character - which include motivational factors, such as a willingness to work for relevant objectives - should rightly determine differences in the education offered. This is a justification, then, for the existence of different types of schools, including specialist academies for those with particular talents, for instance, in the arts. However, there is no reason why requirements such as these should not be met within a state-supplied system of education. It remains to consider how far another factor, the wishes of parents and their ability to pay, should affect the education children receive. The existence of an option to provide a formally organised education in privately financed schools is resisted on grounds which differ significantly from the grounds on which greater equality within the state's system is advocated. The principle of paying for *some* elements of education - swimming lessons, music tuition, tennis coaching - is in general unquestioned, but payment for the central core of education is seen as an infringement of the rights of others. Where the schools concerned are small and are of no particular standing, then parents who choose to make use of them may be seen as no worse than misguided - snobbish, perhaps, and a social irritant, but hardly immoral. Where the major independent institutions are concerned, however, with their high prestige and reputation for efficiency and academic success, then the opposition aroused is of a different order entirely. Here the charges are that privilege is being purchased, and that because of the generally assumed correlation of academic success in youth with material success (wealth, power and influence) later in life, a procedure comparable to the purchase of the rotten boroughs is being engaged in by those who make use of the system.

In considering the issue, there are several questions which need to be resolved. First the exact nature of the egalitarian case against independent schools needs to be examined, and the factual assumptions on which this case is based need to be established. If, as a result of this process, it emerges that there is indeed a practical gain for some at the practical expense of others, then a moral issue will have been exposed, and the debate must inevitably proceed by the weighing of moral considerations. In particular, it must be considered whether there are any other moral principles relevant to the issue apart from that of equality, and if so, what their relative weighting must be.

The egalitarian case for the abolition of the independent sector has been developed in the course of the present century in various types of publication, but particularly in the British context in such sources as Fabian Society pamphlets and Labour Party policy documents, rather than in sources of an overtly or consciously philosophical nature. As a political objective, the aim of the abolition of the private sector did not appear very early as a tenet of socialist policy. This is understandable since in the early days of socialism it would have been a natural assumption that education was a purchasable commodity, and that the objective for socialists must be to provide the purchase-price for those unable to provide it for themselves. It is also the case that the idea of compulsory state education could never have been a serious contender for adoption as a practical policy until the machinery of the modern state had developed to a point at which it was practically possible for a state to supply buildings, teachers and administrators on a scale sufficient to encompass the needs of the entire child population. This has, as a matter of fact, coincided with the rise of socialism, and thus explains to some extent the correlation of socialist policies of educational improvement in the state sector with attacks on the existence of a private sector, particularly where, as in the case of the English public schools, or certain prestige establishments in the United States, that private sector provides a yardstick against which the standards of the state schools can be monitored and measured.[1]

First, then, it may be agreed that financial and fiscal arrangements in most developed countries are such that it would today be a practical possibility for the state to supply the educational needs of the entire child population of these countries. In some countries the state does indeed do so, and there is thus what Mill termed a state monopoly of education. The question then turns, not on the possibility, but on the desirability of such an arrangement.

The first element of the case against private education is of a highly general nature, and derives from a yet more general position which amounts, in effect, to a basic moral objection to the private provision of whatever is vital to a man's well-being, whether education, health, or some less significant commodity. In order to grasp the basis of this objection, it is necessary to ask whether any violation of this principle would occur if the commodity purchased were recognisably identical to that which the state could provide, for the objection might be thought to depend on the factual assumption that money buys a *superior* commodity - better or more prompt health care or hospital treatment; a statistically greater chance of good examination grades or a place at a university. On the other hand, it might be thought that what money provides is not necessarily something superior in quality, but simply a possibility of choice. In this case, the question arises as to whether the original objection would still hold if choice could be built into state provision too. Of course, if the choice referred to is *between* private and state-provided resources, then this elimination of private resources would necessarily eliminate choice. There are those, however, who would object to the private provision of education and key commodities in general even if it were shown that the privately supplied product was in important respects inferior to that which the state could supply. In the case of private education, factors mentioned in support of this sort of adverse assessment of the product are factors concerned with social mix, or the development of skills and knowledge other than the purely academic.

Since any one of these positions may be held by objectors to private education, and since the basic objections may be sustained whether the schools are considered better, worse, or on a par, it follows that there is a ground for opposition which is not based on an imputation of privilege or unfair advantage, but on something more fundamental. Since it is not based on the nature of the product, it must rest on the origin of the provision, and this means that in the last resort it must rest on an overwhelming preference for the state as provider in preference to the private individual or organisation. This basic ideological stance will be considered again in a later chapter. At this point the more specific arguments will be examined and in approaching these it will be useful to return to the distinction made in the previous chapter between two types of egalitarianism. One of these forms of egalitarianism has as its aim a situation in which what is agreed to be good should be extended to everyone; minimum standards should be met for all, on this view, but it will not be necessary as a matter of principle, to secure the elimination of privileges the elimination of which cannot materially improve the standards of anyone else. A second kind of egalitarianism, on the other hand, involves promotion of equality for its own sake; the elimination of privileges will be, for an egalitarian of this type, good in itself, whether it has any advantageous effects for others or not, and even, possibly, if it has deleterious effects.

In the light of this distinction, it is significant to note that up to the time of the Second World War the socialist aim was that major private institutions should be available to all - rather than that they should be eliminated. This was to be achieved either through a generous scholarship system which would literally open such schools to the poor working class; or through massive improvements in state schools, which would make them indistinguishable in quality from famous independent schools. Such objectives - or objectives so expressed - would be unthinkable in the political climate of the present day. Instead, the objective of supplying avenues to these schools has become, by an easy transition, that of integrating such schools into the state system. This transition, though easy, is none the less a significant reversal of direction, since in effect and in outcome it is impossible to distinguish the objective of full integration from that of abolition. The distinction between the two aims is purely semantic.

The arguments of those who favour such a course, when not based on an ideological objection to non-state provision, fall into certain distinct categories. There is first of all opposition to privilege; and the imputation of privilege may be grounded on assumptions about the conditions of schooling (better facilities, more and better teachers within the schools) or about the future occupations of those who have attended independent schools. Closely linked to this are arguments about elitism, whether of wealth, social class, or intellect. These arguments tend to spring from a concentration on the social engineering functions of education, and from a point of view which sees schools as a microcosm of society which might be made to reflect what the larger society *ought* to be, rather than what it is or can be. The social segregation which results from the existence of expensive fee-paying schools outside the state system has, indeed, been described as a form of 'educational apartheid'. Finally, there are a group of fact-based objections not so much to independence, but to the boarding element, which is, particularly in Britain, a concomitant (though not a universal) feature of the system. It is here that charges about the emotional and developmental effects of boarding-schools appear, and in particular the charges of encouraging latent homosexuality. Here the nature of boarding-schools as closed communities exercising tight control over their members is stressed. In addition there are arguments concerning taxation and resources which are based on objections to the charitable status of the schools and the degree of fiscal leniency that this entails. Finally, there are arguments of a more impressionistic nature put forward by those who favour efficiency and modernity, and accuse the schools of fostering amateurism rather than professionalism and of being biased in favour of the arts, particularly classics, as opposed to science and technology.

As far as the arguments concerning matters of fact are concerned, it is sufficient here to point out that the facts claimed are by no means beyond dispute. Advocates of boarding education, far from conceding that there are adverse personality effects resulting from it, would claim character development as a principal benefit of the system. The charges of immaturity and emotional retardation would be balanced by claims of social poise, self-confidence and reliability. That the products of, for example, English public schools are more highly represented in the world of homosexuals than a control group of similar people otherwise educated would also be denied, and the point can certainly not be carried by arbitrary personal observation. The accusation of an arts bias would be countered by the alternative portrayal favoured by the schools themselves of adaptation to changing requirements and high levels of attainment in scientific and mathematical fields. The taxation and resource arguments are of a highly technical nature, but it is worth noticing that arguments for redistribution of resources on these grounds often proceed on the false assumption that the resources involved, both human and physical, are readily redistributable, whereas, of course, the abolition of fee-paying out of private after-tax income must inevitably result in a net loss of funds to education. The students themselves would become an additional burden on state funds, and as for the buildings and grounds, desirable though these may appear when compared with the resources of some inner city schools, they are largely sited in inaccessible rural areas, rendering any redistribution of their acres and facilities entirely theoretical.

More important than these technical considerations are the political and moral points underlying the first group of arguments, which again involve reference to some matters of fact. The first arguments mentioned were those concerned with privilege and elitism. As far as the question of superior facilities and staffing is concerned, it must be admitted that parents may well expect advantages in these respects in return for their patronage. However, the facts are not so clear-cut. Facilities of state schools are often superior, certainly in terms of modernity, to those of all but the best-endowed of private schools, and staffing ratios are strictly comparable when like is compared with like. Boarding-schools provide round-the-clock care and therefore need a different staffing ratio from day-schools. Comparisons should therefore be between state and private boarding-schools, or between state and private day-schools.[2]

Nevertheless, it is undeniable that the prevailing opinion is that these schools on the whole provide their users with a better start in life than comparable state schools. The objection underlying charges of privilege based on this assumption is often based on a competitive rather than co-operative view of society. Certain occupations and lifestyles are seen as rewards or prizes and, in the interest of fairness, it is implied that the race for these prizes must be run from an equal starting-point. No one must be allowed - in the first few laps at least - to gain a start which it will be difficult for anyone lacking that advantage to make up.

One practical objection to this position is that it is in many obvious ways a recipe for mediocrity - and mediocrity is not in the interests of society nor, therefore, in the interest of the individuals making up society, whether they themselves enjoy the privilege or not. For instance, it was in the interest of society in general that Mozart should have had a specially advantageous musical background and education, even if, as is undoubtedly the case, many other potentially talented musicians fell by the wayside for lack of encouragement or adequate tuition and opportunities. If it is argued that Mozart's talent was so exceptional that he would have achieved what he did in spite of every obstacle, then it must be admitted that many lesser individuals, whose contribution has nevertheless been valuable, have been dependent on early encouragement, and others, of whom nothing is known, have been deterred by its absence. Nineteenth-century factories and mines were undoubtedly places where much potential talent in many cultural fields failed to flourish. In attempting to eliminate unfair early advantages, it would meet the reasonable aims of very few fair-minded people if a monolithic and equality-oriented state system of education became the twentieth-century equivalent of those factories and mines, fulfilling the same function of talent suppression.

Some writings on this theme, however, give the impression that this is indeed the aim. H. Glennerster, writing on the subject of education and inequality, said: 'True democracy is incompatible with wide extremes of wealth or *attainment*' (my italics).[3] This surprisingly stark statement prompts the response that any society we can conceive of will require wide varieties of attainment, if only in the sense of specialisation. It is not merely undesirable, but patently impossible, that every child should play the piano, or do algebra or gymnastics, at more or less the same level. But if differences of attainment in these areas are to be unquestioned, it is difficult to show why diversity of intellectual attainment in the sense in which this can be measured by public examinations and university entrance should be ruled out on ideological grounds. Indeed, it is difficult to recognise as a moral point of view one that would suppress advantage simply because advantage - virtually by definition - cannot be universally shared. It follows, then, that if some independent schools do specially cultivate and foster intellectual talent, then the argument against early advantage is based on weak moral grounds. A morally sounder alternative course would be to eliminate the advantage by improving the response of the state sector to children's intellectual potential.

The charge of privilege, however, may involve reference to something beyond the quality of the education offered. It may stem, indeed, from reflections on the statistical distribution of those who have attended the schools - and particularly some of the major prestige establishments - in key occupations (for example, law and politics) which, taken together, represent the power-structure of society. It is here that charges of privilege merge into charges of elitism, and the schools are seen as the means by which is created an elite, whether of wealth, intellect, or social class. There is, however, an imperfect correlation of these last three factors. Whilst a certain level of income may be a necessary condition for use of the schools, the social class of those who meet this condition is not invariable. These two factors taken together correlate even more imperfectly with intellectual ability, and the charge that an intellectual hierarchy or caste system is being created is very much less plausible than that there is a hierarchy based on wealth or social class.

The two charges of privilege and elitism cannot be taken entirely in isolation from each other, however. For if the prestigious occupational roles in question are roles for which a high standard of education is required, and if the charge that the schools provide a particularly high standard of education is accepted, then this apparent over-representation is to be expected. But even if the figures on the educational backgrounds of influential groups were to be construed as establishing the existence of a hereditary elite based on social class, rather than on the quality of the education offered, it must be asked whether the social engineering aim of the elimination of this class should be approached through the manipulation of educational arrangements. Since education itself is compulsory, how far should this widely accepted interference with the freedom of both children and parents be taken over for socio-political ends? If it is not simply education, but the time and place of education, which are specified by the state - with the ultimate sanction of the legal removal of a child from his parents' care if they refuse to comply - then individual freedom is something that will apply for most individuals only during the few years that elapse between leaving school and re-encountering the educational system a few years later as a parent. If a state is able to dominate its citizens' lives to this extent, then its claim to be a free society will be very limited indeed. To place in the hands of any government, no matter how benevolent, the means by which it - and therefore its less predictable successors - may control the lives and minds of its citizens by placing them for the entire impressionable portion of their lives in designated compulsory establishments is to gamble with the future. Fictional representations of youth movements in which children and teenagers denounce their parents for subversive tendencies have had too many historical and contemporary non-fictitious parallels for the possibility to be ignored.[4] What is at stake in discussion of the creation of a state monopoly of education - the abolition of the private sector - is nothing less than the setting-up of the machinery for this kind of macabre development.

The counter to such talk of freedom is very frequently to point out that for the overwhelming majority of people there is in fact no escape from the ubiquitous embrace of state education, and that the financial constraints within which most families operate effectively rule out recourse to the non-state alternative. This may be so. But in any case, while there is a widely accepted principle that some things are so important to a human being's welfare that access to them should not be denied from lack of money - and education certainly falls into this category - there is no general principle acknowledged in a democratic society against anyone owning or purchasing what may be beyond the means of some.

However, whatever the economic facts, and even if the most unfavourable hypothesis is adopted and it is assumed that very few people can opt for schools outside the state system, it is a perverse construction of 'freedom' to suggest that the remainder do not therefore have freedom in respect of education, or that their freedom would be the same whether or not a non-state alternative existed. On the contrary, their freedom in relation to the state system is entirely dependent on the existence of an alternative. The existence of a freedom does not depend upon its actual exercise, nor is it even necessary that a lesser demand should be satisfied: that it should be possible for the freedom to be universally and simultaneously exercised. For example, freedom to dine at the Ritz or to take a world cruise is not dependent, as is often suggested, on whether one can in fact, or whether one does in fact, do either of these things; nor does it depend on whether there would be room for all in the restaurant or on the ship. As Hirsch has recently argued, there may be social constraints on freedom in the sense that the very exclusiveness of some activities (for example, owning an isolated country cottage) depends on the limited numbers of those seeking these goods, but although widespread demand might make these particular goods unobtainable, it is a mistake to see this as setting a limit to freedom. Our freedom may be subject to practical limitations, but possibility rather than actuality sets the boundaries of freedom.[5]

Not only is it unnecessary for a potential freedom to be actualised, but in the case of most freedoms their simultaneous and universal actualisation is, paradoxically, impossible. For example, one may consider a small closed self-sufficient community, each member of which receives a certain income and for whom each week a certain range of goods is available for purchase. Each individual is free to purchase any of the goods, but no individual will be free to purchase all. The second point does not, however, invalidate the first. The freedom of the individual members is not confined to the purchases they actually make. It is the rule, then, rather than the exception, for freedom to be concerned with selection or choice rather than with actual possession; and it is simply a fact of life that each individual choice, once made, automatically excludes its multiple alternatives.

It is therefore absurd to argue in respect of education that the freedom to purchase private education is dependent upon actually buying it, rather than upon having it available as an option. Those who buy and those who do not buy are equally free, and their freedom cannot be constrained by personal circumstances, as long as their formal freedom to purchase remains. Closing down this option, however, would involve the absurdity of attempting to rectify a situation in which some were deemed unfree (for economic reasons) by one in which all would be rendered unfree. Any gain in such a situation would have to be seen, then, in other terms altogether.

For some people the issue of freedom will be the decisive consideration in this controversy, and because of its importance will merit separate discussion later. At this point it will be useful, rather than pursuing these important theoretical concerns, to point briefly to some purely practical gains which accrue as a result of the existence of a private sector to those who, whether from choice or personal necessity, themselves use the state sector of education. The existence of establishments which are entirely consumer-oriented - because in order to survive they must satisfy their clients - provides a measure of what is wanted which can be constantly held up against what is supplied in less consumer-responsive organisations. This has been illustrated in debates over both the content of the curriculum and methods of teaching. On the whole what seems to have emerged is that parents as consumers of education are traditional and conservative in their aspirations. In the main the private sector reflects these aspirations, but at the same time reflects, too, the existence of a small group of parents whose demand is for a freer, more creative approach. In the private sector the latter demand is met in separate establishments which are then chosen for these qualities - both parents and children, as well as their teachers, know what will be offered.

Schools which radically change their character with a change of head, or even with a change of attitude on the part of the existing head, are a feature of the sector which provides compulsory customers. Without the existence of the independent yardstick, the temptation to argue that what people are getting is what they want might be even greater than it is.

Practical considerations alone cannot, however, determine this issue. Freedoms are more readily eroded or abolished than reinstated. The fundamental point that has been argued here is that the debate about independent education is not a matter of weighing the interests of the majority, in respect of equality, against the few, in respect of freedom; but that everyone's interests are affected in both respects. But before turning to the general issues of freedom, choice and independence, it would be useful to pause and consider the position of those who see the rights and freedoms of parents in respect of education as being in conflict with the rights and freedoms of children.

NOTES: CHAPTER 3

1 Although the British Labour Party called for the 'nationalisation' of education in 1918 (Labour Party, *Labour and the New Social Order,* London, 1918), this was not interpreted as a call for the abolition of the private sector - a demand which was not in fact explicitly formulated until after the Second World War, nor adopted as policy until 1961 in the Labour Party manifesto *Signposts for the Sixties.*
2 The conclusion arrived at on this issue in G. Kalton, *The Public Schools: A Factual Survey* (London: Longman, 1966), after close comparison of staffing ratios in various types of schools in Great Britain, is that when allowance is made for numbers of sixth-formers 'the differences between public schools and their equivalent category of maintained school almost disappear' (p. 66).
3 H. Glennerster, 'Education and inequality', in P. Townsend and N. Bosanquet, *Labour and Inequality* (London: Fabian Society, 1972), p. 77.
4 The best-known fictional example of this is in George Orwell's *1984.*
5 F. Hirsch, *Social Limits to Growth* (London: Routledge & Kegan Paul, 1976).

Chapter 4

Parents and Children

If parents are permitted to express their personal viewpoint, bias or even eccentricity in the educational arrangements they make for their children, either in terms of choice of school or perhaps even by opting out of formal education altogether, then the question must be raised of whether they are in fact exercising their own preference at the expense of equally important rights and freedoms belonging to their children. Once this point of view is considered, it becomes clear that the state could be seen as the champion and protector of children's rights against their parents.

The case of those who choose schools outside the state system has been considered in the preceding chapter, and since most schools, whatever their orientation, attempt to comply, if only for commercial and practical reasons, with some recognised norms of education, it is unlikely that a child will be entirely deprived of his right to develop freely as an educated member of society as a result of his parents' choice in these cases. Even if his school upbringing encourages him to adopt a minority position, such as vegetarianism or an extreme form of right-wing conservatism, the public and open nature of the influence is such that he is as likely to react against his upbringing later in life as to continue in line with it. This is not so clearly the case, though, where the private and domestic nature of purely parental upbringing is concerned. It is important, therefore, to consider the case of the several hundred children each year whose parents adopt a more radical option than choosing a private school, and for a variety of reasons refuse schooling altogether on their children's behalf.

In order to illustrate the variety of grounds on which this choice may be based, it will be useful to take for consideration a number of fictional cases. It should be stressed that while no real families are referred to here, names and backgrounds having been arbitrarily assigned, the actual elements of the situations do represent reality.

SEVEN FAMILIES

(a) The Brown parents are believers in what has come to be called Victorian morality. They favour a simple life and consider that schools today are, as Ivan Illich and his supporters claim, the advertising agencies of the consumer society. Schools also, in the Browns' view, purvey a slipshod and permissive conception of morality. To protect their children from these morally damaging influences, the Browns, who are themselves well-educated middle-class parents, are prepared to educate their children at home.

(*b*) This view of the moral atmosphere of state schools is shared by the White parents, who are Muslims wishing to educate their daughters at a single-sex school. As the state provides only mixed schools in their area and they cannot afford the cost of private education, they prefer to keep their daughters at home, although they do not claim to be able themselves to supply an alternative education for them. Education, however, in their view, must take second place to morality and cultural tradition.

(*c*) The Greens, on the other hand, far from seeing the state schools as morally permissive, see them as restrictive, and seek to provide their children with a far more open, Rousseau-inspired education. They are themselves educationists and believers in self-expression and dis-covery-based learning, and they consider themselves best qualified to provide such an education for their children. Attitudes to nudity and sex education will be a significant aspect for their personally devised programme, as will an absence of religious education.

(*d*) The case of the Greys is different, in that the Grey children all attended primary school without significant problems. The Grey parents, however, object to the principle of comprehensive education and are prepared to keep their children at home unless and until some alternative is offered them. Like the Whites, they are not in a financial position to pay for education in the private sector, although there are independent schools which they would find acceptable.

(*e*) The Plum children also attended primary school, and their parents would be happy for them to attend the popular comprehensive school in their locality. However, education in the large city in which they live is organised in such a way that, in order to achieve what the authority considers to be a 'balanced intake' in their comprehensive schools, their children have been assigned to a school in a rundown area of the city, known to suffer from problems of violence and indiscipline, where academic achievement is low and which, in addition, involves a lengthy bus journey. The Plums have joined with other dissatisfied parents in employing a teacher on premises they have jointly rented, and intend to keep their children away from school until they are offered a satisfactory solution.

(*f*) The Scarlet children have themselves played truant from school on many occasions and their parents, who share their low view of academic education, are happy for them to attend the new Free School which has been set up in their area by some idealistic young teachers in sympathy with the anti-establishment subculture of the Scarlets and others in the area. The Free School makes no rules regarding hours of attendance or work to be undertaken. For this reason, the Scarlets are not considered by the education authority to be providing alternative schooling for their children, but to be in the same situation as others who refuse school.

(g) Finally, there are the Blacks, whose children seem extremely talented in various directions - musical, mathematical, artistic - and who attribute this to the education policies they have adopted from birth. They feel that conventional schooling can only harm their children and that they can arrange the right opportunities for their children from the home base, from either their own resources, libraries, or tutors.

The children of these seven families, do not form by any means a homogeneous group. Some have been found to be backward in reading and basic skills, while others are proficient in several languages or display mathematical or artistic brilliance. Some are judged socially isolated and maladjusted, while others, by contrast, are mature and adult in their approach to the adults who interview or examine them; some may be deemed sexually uniformed, others sexually precocious; some express strong religious conviction, others assume atheism, or have never engaged their minds on religious issues.

The one common factor, indeed, is that all the children display a ferocious loyalty to their parents and to the choice which their parents have made on their behalf. They see organised society, through their contacts with social workers or local officials, as fundamentally antagonistic to the close-knit family group which at least until adolescence commands their first loyalty. Amongst the parents, on the other hand, there are those who wish the state to comply with their expectations and those whose strong individualism requires of the state only non-interference. Many of these cases provoke the keenest controversy and require resolution one way or another. In some cases a benefactor or a small concession in policy on the part of the authorities will solve the problem, though there may well be a strong feeling on the part of onlookers that these *deus ex machina* solutions are unfair to those who have themselves objected to arrangements but have nevertheless complied. A different objection is that such *ad hoc* solutions in fact enable people to avoid facing up to the issues of principle involved, and it is to these issues therefore that it will be appropriate to turn next.

The British system is in fact remarkably tolerant in respect of families wishing to find alternatives to formally arranged education. The relevant section of the 1944 Education Act states:

> It shall be the duty of the parent of every child of compulsory school age to cause him to receive efficient full-time education suitable to his age, ability, and aptitude, either by regular attendance at school or otherwise.[1]

Nevertheless, it is clear that the concession implied in the words 'or otherwise' cannot be taken as authorising *any* departure from normal practice, since it would, for example, be unreasonable to permit parents to use this clause in order to keep their children at home as domestic slaves. Nor can the children's own present wishes necessarily be taken as decisive, for even in cases where children have been the victims of brutal and violent treatment from a parent, they have been known to express a preference for remaining at home under such circumstances rather than being taken into institutional care. Inevitably, therefore, the problem must be recognised as one of compromise, or drawing a line between parental authority and children's interests as seen by the rest of society.

There is a parallel here with the position of conscientious objectors in war. Conscientious objectors are permitted to do what it would be impossible for everyone to be allowed to do. To begin with, the strength of their conviction is recognised to be such as to make compulsion ineffectual, and secondly, the number of people who can be found genuinely to have such convictions is so small as to make no difference to the overall situation. Similarly, the task of compelling a tiny minority of objectors to state education is one which the liberal state may find both unattractive and unnecessary. Nevertheless, it is important that the basic moral position is made clear, so that decisions are made with these principles consciously in view.

The situation is one which involves both rights and duties. Of the three parties involved, both parents and children may be acknowledged to have rights. The rights of parents are expressed in terms of an appeal to the principle of liberty; those of children in their claim not only to share the freedom of their parents, but also to educational development - to be equipped to participate in the adult society of which they must ultimately form a part. The state's intervention is justified not in terms of *its* rights, but those of children who need to be adequately safeguarded against neglectful or ill-intentioned parents, and it can therefore be expressed in terms of the notion of duty. The notion of duty on the part of the state cannot be understood precisely analogously to that of a duty on the part of an individual, but nevertheless there is a long tradition to the idea that the state has obligations towards its citizens, which in part account for their reciprocal obligations to obey the state. (Such an argument was in fact advanced by Socrates in Plato's dialogue, the *Crito*, to justify his refusal to attempt to avoid his own legally ordered execution.) It is reasonable, then, to attribute to the state a duty in respect of children's education, which does provide a *prima facie* justification for state interference, but the precise interpretation of this duty will need further consideration.

First, however, recognition of the state's duty must be balanced by the recognition that parents also have a duty with regard to the education and upbringing of their children. Indeed, it is this duty that forms the ground of their rights. Many people claim not to be able to understand talk about rights, whilst being perfectly willing to talk about duties and obligations. While the wider justification of rights must be left until later, it can be said at this point that anyone who is prepared to subscribe to the view that someone *ought* to do something is logically committed to the belief that that person has a *right* to do that action. It would, in other words, be self-contradictory to assert that 'A ought to do X' and also that 'A has no right to do X'. Unlike statements about what is right or wrong, good or bad, statements about duties and obligations are essentially closed recommendations to a single course of action, and this course of action must be one that is both practically and morally possible. That something that ought to be done must be *practically* possible has long been recognised, but its *moral* possibility - in the sense that it must be morally right or appropriate - is equally important. It is for this reason that talk about duties necessarily generates talk about rights. If someone has a duty to do something, then he has also a right to do it. If he has no right, then he cannot be held to have a duty.

Being a parent, then, involves both rights and obligations and, if it is more than a merely biological relationship, has moral and emotional aspects. This is not to suggest, however, that these aspects actually define the parent-child relationship, as would be argued by those who claim that family obligations follow from the nature of the family as a social institution, and that constitutive rules define offices and roles within the family. Those who subscribe to this type of view would say that just as being chairman of a political meeting, or wicket-keeper in a cricket match, can be defined in terms of what one ought to do in the meeting or in the cricket-match, and how others ought to behave towards the chairman or wicket-keeper, so being a parent or son or daughter is at the least partly definable in such terms.

It is not unreasonable to extend such an interpretation from quasi-political institutions to some social institutions and to institutions such as that of promising, where being a promisor or promisee can best be understood in terms of relative obligations. Where the institution of the family is concerned, however, A. I. Melden's criticism of this type of interpretation is effective in demonstrating that the unwritten rules of family life are not comparable to the constitutive rules of political associations or of sport and games.[2] For a constitutive rule actually defines a term - expands, for instance, what it *is* to be chairman or wicket-keeper. It says nothing about a person's moral performance in that role. So the moral obligations of family members do not *define* what it is to be parent, child, husband, or wife. It is possible to *be* any of these things and altogether neglect the obligations involved. Melden points out, too, that the respective obligations of parents and children change as children progress from infancy to maturity, so that the idea of a single set of constitutive rules is untenable, and a successively changing set implausible.

Nevertheless, family membership is not fully explained and understood in purely biological terms. If this were so the ethical and legal problems in relation to adoption, illegitimacy, artificial insemination and test-tube babies would not be as complex as they are. The moral and emotional aspects of parenthood, then, are extremely important. And amongst the former, the duty to care for, bring up and in the most fundamental sense educate one's children compel acknowledgement.

From an evolutionary point of view the survival of the human species to the point where, as now, the state could in principle take over the parental role has depended on at least minimal acceptance of this obligation. Even in the case of the Ik - an East African tribe whose social relationships broke down on the loss of their traditional hunting-grounds, and whose experience is vividly described by Colin Turnbull - supports this contention.[3] For although child-parent relationships had apparently broken down completely, with children forming themselves into self-sustaining groups, two or three years of maternal care still remained the norm, even in this extreme case. Acknowledgement of such duties, then, has until the present century, with its vastly increased resources and high degree of centralised organisation, been necessary for survival. But practical utility does not make morality; it merely inclines the recalcitrant to accept it. And, indeed, it is because the moral bond between parents and children is essentially independent of considerations of utility that the fact that surrounding circumstances have changed does not alter the essence of that relationship.

Parents, then, do have rights in respect of the education of their children, which arise from their duty to provide for them reaching maturity and the kind of independence that social circumstances make necessary. But this observation suggests that the state's duty in this respect is a much more sophisticated concept. Indeed, since the state is not a person, it is only by an anthropomorphic analogy that it can be said to have duties. In the case of bringing up children, reference to the duty of the state can best be understood as a reference to the duty of other members of society acting collectively to take the place of parents where they are unable or unwilling to fulfil those duties themselves. So understood it is clear that while this duty does exist, and does generate a corresponding right, it is merely a residual duty and a residual right. Once this is recognised, some light is thrown on the problem-cases described earlier, although there is still room for disagreement on matters which are, in the last resort, matters of judgement.

Those who would unquestioningly recommend administrative coercion, though, should see that the weight of principle is in favour of the parental dissident and not in favour of compulsion, difficult though this may be to perceive for anyone nurtured in the ubiquitous embrace of the modern state. Moreover, since the state's intervention is justified in terms of what it would be right for other members of society to do, it cannot be the case that the state has rights which its individual members could not have. It may therefore act as in a smaller community a group of neighbours having the interests of a child at heart might legitimately act - rescuing the child who risks death at the hands of a violent parent, for example, or educating and caring for the child whose parents are dead or have deserted him. But where such a group of neighbours would hesitate to intervene, there ought the organised state to hesitate also.

Hence the sincere convictions of at least the first three of the parents of the families cited as examples, which would provoke precisely this kind of neighbourly hesitation and respect for an alternative moral perspective, provide a case where the state should stand aside, even though it may judge the viewpoint of the parents to be mistaken or misguided. In the case of the Blacks the misjudgement of the parents may be much clearer to demonstrate, the success of their children in particular spheres be easier to recognise objectively, and the issue could therefore turn on the factual question of whether the children, if prodigies, are achieving the level of performance of their potential.

The remaining cases are as controversial as the position of conscientious objectors who object, not to war in general, but to a particular war, since these parents object, not to schools, but to the schools they have been offered. They in fact reflect the powerlessness of the individual to influence the character of a system, and as a protest against this impotence deserve to be treated with some tolerance. Nevertheless, it is understandable that this tolerance should be strained, if it appears to result in the state making a concession to some that it is unwilling to make in the case of others. Here it is notions of fairness, not equality, that generate the strain.

Nevertheless, the principle of respecting parental rights and recognising the inviolability of the family in all but the most clear-cut of cases is strong enough to justify acceptance of occasional cases of unfairly preferential treatment. For where two inflexible forces meet - determined parents and the power of the state as represented by local authority officials - the application of the state's ultimate sanction of removing children from their home and taking them into institutional care must result in greater unfairness still to the children involved in the dispute. There is no doubt that the state is more powerful than the individual and can win these encounters, but for this very reason it should be cautious in adopting such a strategy.

The case of the Free School family makes this point even more clearly. Their protest is essentially one against coercion. To counter such a protest with coercion is both psychologically undesirable and politically unsound. To take the psychological aspect first, it is undeniable that not every child or young person can fit happily into the straitjacket of formal education. Some adolescents develop school phobia - a condition which, while it may be treated with scepticism by some medical or educational personnel, is none the less real in its physical and emotional manifestations. Ill-directed pressure in these cases can produce extremely distressing results ranging from physical sickness to attempted suicide and suicide. For families with problems of this nature, a Free School can be a saving solution. It is even more likely to be this in the case of truancy following the pattern of the Scarlet example, and as a solution may be favoured by educational authorities themselves. For even parents who object to their children's truancy may be powerless to control the activities of a teenage son or daughter, particularly if they have jobs or commitments of their own at the relevant hours. For these kinds of reasons, then, the case of parents who prefer to allow their children to attend a Free School, even where this means a repudiation of conventional standards of attainment or behaviour, is likely to be more sympathetically viewed than some of the other cases cited.

But the political aspect of this situation is even more compelling. The reluctance of the liberal state to intervene when what is at issue is a protest against coercion is not an accidental feature of such a state, but is in fact part of what the notion of a liberal state involves. It is particularly in its encounters with the family that a liberal state will display such hesitation. For the family represents one of the few forces within society powerful enough to resist the encroachments of a state drifting towards authoritarianism. This fact has been recognised by advocates of totalitarianism, who from Plato onwards have combined policies of state domination of the individual's life with policies designed to undermine the influence of family ties. The day-nursery and the creche, while desirable for all kinds of other reasons, can in the hands of a government thirsty for domination of the minds of its citizens be powerful instruments of control.

But even within the liberal state, there may be arguments for qualifying the authority of the parent by external constraints. Such arguments have been extensively discussed, for example, in connection with the Amish communities of the United States. Amish children are born into membership of a centuries-old religious group - a group which is self-sufficient in farming and makes virtually no demands on the rest of the community. The concession sought by Amish parents was that their children should be excused the last two years of compulsory schooling in the ordinary American high school. Principally in order to protect freedom of religion, legal opinion favoured this exemption.[4] But considering this and similar cases, Kenneth Henley has produced an argument which, if successful, would completely destroy the case for family freedom which has been argued above.

Henley[5] sees the authority to educate as being based on the child's own need to be educated for the sake of a more satisfying life - a position from which few would dissent. He goes on to claim, however, that while the child needs his family relationships when young, he also needs external school relationships to facilitate his independence from his family as he matures. Henley quotes the American Supreme Court's recognition of the 'liberty of parents and guardians to direct the upbringing and education of children under their control' but he argues that

(1) the right to religious freedom must be protected against parental pressure,
(2) the child must not be intentionally isolated from contact with other religions and ways of life and therefore
(3) the child has a right to attend a *state* school.

This is a right which he maintains must be upheld even against the wishes of a parent, and possibly the wishes of the child himself. In itself the notion of a right which can be forced on one against one's will is paradoxical. Henley, moreover, sees this right as one which could be violated even by attendance at a private school, if this is not state-approved, and state approval he sees as depending not on academic matters, but on whether the school admits children of all racial, ethnic and religious backgrounds. Even the content of the teaching is, in Henley's opinion, subject to state approval and, for instance, he considers that this would be rightly withheld if science teaching was based on a rejection of Darwin. In this connection it is interesting to note that the famous 'monkey trial' in the United States, in which a teacher was prosecuted for teaching Darwinian evolutionary theory instead of the fundamentalist Christian doctrine of the creation, has had a recent parallel in England with the dismissal of a fundamentalist Christian teacher from a state school for insisting on teaching Darwinism as a possible rather than a confirmed theory.

The highly contentious question of religious belief will be discussed more fully in the next chapter, but its relevance to the question at present under discussion - the clash between parental and state authority - is very clear. While the object of the autonomy of children - the aim that they should be allowed to mature into independent adults with their own view of life - is extremely compelling, the argument for autonomy cannot be allowed to range through Henley's three stages. If it does so, it would permit an all-powerful state to deny autonomy to adults on the pretext of guaranteeing that of children. Apart from the fact that neither culture nor religion can survive generational jumps, but, as the Amish recognised, must be allowed to span the generations without interruption, the argument as presented assumes the possibility of a wholly reasonable, wholly uncontentious form of educational provision, which it could be nobody's right to refuse. If this were a possibility, then the case for protecting the child against parental pressure might be stronger. But it is not so, as the seven fictional cases, representative of many genuine cases, make clear.

Nevertheless, a parent who, convinced of the rightness of his own point of view, attempts to shield his child from contact with all other viewpoints, is indeed, on a personal level, doing his child a disservice. However, in objecting to this, it is necessary to consider the alternative. This can only be that the state should compulsorily supply the correct perspective. The reason why it is preferable that the autonomy of the child should be violated in certain cases by his parents is simply that children inevitably grow up and are emancipated from their parents in the course of time. Children are well known to be as likely to react violently against their upbringing as to follow it. Entering the adult world automatically guarantees contact with others whose childhood pressures have been different and whose views have been differently, if equally strongly, shaped. But from the state there is no such emancipation. No automatic process of maturing frees one from the authority of the state. And if a similar, no matter how rational, perspective or point of view has been inculcated by a closely controlled state system of education, no one having been left outside this consensus control, then adult life will bring no rubbing of shoulders with the eccentrically different. The pattern will in fact be set for uniformity and state domination of mind and opinion.

It is almost as important, though, that the state should not institutionalise its permission of dissent. In Germany in the 1930s a system was introduced whereby any group of parents could ask the state to provide them with a school representing their own *Weltanschauung,* or view of life, providing only that they could provide a petition with a dozen signatories. This enabled the Nazi movement to secure schools run according to their own ideals at a pace which could not have occurred without this concession. The moral to be drawn from this is that the state's contribution should be permissive only, and permissive to individuals rather than groups, since for the liberal state it is individualism alone that has value, not the cultivation of organised difference.

NOTES: CHAPTER 4

1 Education Act 1944, s. 36.
2 A. I. Melden, *Rights and Persons* (Oxford: Blackwell, 1977), pp. 69-80.
3 C. Turnbull, *The Mountain People* (London: Pan, 1972).
4 *Wisconsin v. Yoder,* 406 US 205 (1972), printed in O. O'Neill and W. Ruddick (eds), *Having Children* (Oxford: Oxford University Press, 1979), pp. 280-305.
5 Kenneth Henley, 'The authority to educate', in O'Neill and Ruddick (eds), op. cit., pp. 254-64.

Chapter 5

Religious Freedom

The case of the Amish children mentioned in the last chapter illustrates the fact that religion makes demands of its adherents which are, from the point of view of education, unique in their extent and force. No other area of the curriculum is so potentially pervasive in its influence on the lives of those who have fully grasped and accepted its implications. From a political point of view, too, religion is a force which can bring governments or political systems to an end if they are in conflict with it, and, conversely, if allied to a government or political system render it both totally stable and totally dominating of the lives of its citizens.

For these reasons the question of religious education is more fundamental than some contemporary discussions would suggest. It is important not to see the debate about religious education as centring solely on the presence or absence of designated periods on the school timetable. It is important, too, not to see the issue from a totally individualistic point of view, but to recognise its moral, social and political implications. In approaching these, some more theoretic and analytic questions will need to be considered. Of these, the most basic is the question of how religious education is to be understood. The answer to this question may be given in terms of its purpose, with a clear distinction being drawn between those who would see the purpose of religious education as being to inculcate belief or faith, whether or not they base this on a view of religion which sets it apart from other curriculum areas, and those who see its purpose as being merely to inform. Both of these positions can be found to have some advocates in recent discussion of these issues, and each suggests different answers to the consequent questions which arise once fundamentals have been determined. These consequent questions would include such matters as whether separate religious schooling should be permitted; whether religious education has a place in state schools; who should teach it if so; whether any one religion may be assigned a special status; and what limits the rights of adults and of children set to any programme which may be agreed within a particular society. It will also be relevant to consider whether the nature of the society - the political ideals for which it stands - must affect the answers to these further questions.

First, though, it will be useful to identify some possible positions on the more basic issue. Of these, three seem to be particularly influential:

(1) It may be held that the purpose of religious education is to inculcate belief or faith, and that in this respect religious education is unique in the curriculum.

(2) It may be held that belief or faith is to be inculcated, but that this aim is precisely parallel to analogous aims in other teaching areas, comparable, for instance, to creating aesthetic awareness in the study of literature, or generating scientific attitudes in relation to practical problems.

(3) It may be held that the purpose of religious education is merely to inform students of the psychological, sociological and historical facts concerning religion and familiarise them with its literature, the implication being that any goals beyond this involve indoctrination.

The assumption that the first two of these positions have in common, that the purpose of religious education is to instil faith in a particular religion, is an assumption that would be made by adherents of most non-Christian religions as well as by the Catholic Church. Its denial seems to be particularly linked with the individualism and commitment to toleration of certain sections of Protestant Christianity. As practical educational policy the Plowden Report on primary education, tacitly assuming in its British context the background of the established church (and in spite of a dissenting point of view expressed by members of the committee including A. J. Ayer), adopted this assumption, with the statement that 'Children should not be taught to doubt before faith is established'.[1]

The idea that religious education must involve the acquisition of skills and concepts internal to religion, such as prayer and worship, and not merely the learning of facts *about* religion has been defended by Roger Marples.[2] He disputes the notion that it is possible to have a full religious understanding without some degree of commitment - that religion can be adequately understood from the outside. In support of Marples's position one might compare the position of a blind person who decides to make himself an expert in art appreciation, perhaps by following a broadcast course. Such a person could well develop a high level of academic skill in the description and discussion of fine points of aesthetic appraisal, but it would be plausible to claim that without the opportunity to appreciate directly an example of visual beauty, any teaching he received, no matter how efficient, must be hollow in the most significant respect. Being taught the forms of worship without entering into its spirit could well be regarded as a similarly hollow and limited procedure.

The view that religious education involves initiation into religious belief is also shared by W. D. Hudson, who identifies two aspects of the process: (i) theology, in which the student is initiated into religious discourse, including particularly the concept of God, and (ii) devotion, in which religious belief is 'expressed in performative language, which places trust, acknowledges a claim' etc.[3] Hudson's view is that in religious education the student should learn both how to conceive of God, and how to pray and worship, both, however, subject to the qualification of respect for reason and independence of judgement.

If religious education is seen in this light, then the position of a teacher who is an agnostic or uncommitted to the religion in question becomes difficult if not impossible, for it suggests that religion can only be taught from the point of view of an adherent. The idea that students themselves should be considered free to reject or accept their teacher's beliefs becomes equally unacceptable. For the teacher-adherent must aim to produce religious understanding. But religious understanding, it has been suggested by the two writers mentioned above, is not open to the outsider, only to the person prepared to step inside through the doorway of religious belief. But is it impossible to understand religion without either belief or commitment? Or do Marples and Hudson confuse learning facts or techniques with learning attitudes? It could be argued that the comparison with visual art was misleading. Sealey, for example, suggests a comparison with musical education, or sex education, as areas where education does not necessarily involve initiation.[4] In support of his view he quotes the words of Hirst:

> What cannot be part of education . . . would be seeking to develop, say a disposition to worship in that faith, or certain emotions of love of God, when that very disposition, or these emotions, are only a justifiable development, if the religion is accepted by the individual. That acceptance . . . is a personal, private judgement which education, committed to reason alone as it is, has no right to foreclose.[5]

This rejection of the view that religious education essentially involves the transmission of religious belief is presented by Hirst in the context of a distinction between a 'primitive' and a 'sophisticated' view of Christian education. The primitive view is that such education involves the passing on of what is believed to be true and valuable to the next generation. The sophisticated view, on the other hand, is that it involves the passing on to the next generation only of what we can claim to know and understand, and rationally defend on objective grounds. Hirst argues that in history, literature, or even the study of religion a committed approach is incompatible with the standards of scholarship implicit in the sophisticated approach - standards which demand impartial appraisal, 'truth, based on evidence, irrespective of the particular religious beliefs of the scholar'.[6] Hirst's emphasis, then, is on reason and objectivity in teaching, and as far as religion is concerned he claims that 'no particular substantive religious claims can be either assumed to be, or simply taught as, objectively acceptable'.[7] From this he draws the conclusion that in a secular society the schools which that society finances should not be partisan for any one religion, but should be secular and open institutions.

These two very different views of the nature of religious education - one favouring commitment, the other impartiality - clearly depend closely upon the assumptions made about the status of religion itself. Underlying the discussion is the difference between a view of religion as an area where rational standards apply, or as an area of faith divorced from reason; an area of objective fact or of subjective judgement. It would, however, be a mistake to accept this dichotomy and the arguments dependent on it too hastily. For what it requires is an ability to distinguish between what is true, and what we merely believe or claim to be true. But whereas an onlooker could make that distinction about someone else's beliefs (although it would be in terms of his own beliefs and perceptions), we ourselves can make no such distinction. From our own point of view what is true and what we believe or claim to be true are indistinguishable. The position of those who insist on such a distinction being made in the case of religious belief is therefore not a matter of separating objective truth and subjective judgement, although it is often presented in this way. Instead, underlying it can usually be found a claim about the respectability or acceptability of different types of evidence. The grounds for religious belief are unlikely to be either scientific or logical, and if it is claimed that only scientific or logical grounds can engender certainty, then the uncertainty of religious belief must follow. But a believer need not be led to such conclusions. If scientific or logical methods of proof are inappropriate for what he believes, then he may hold that since what he believes is true, there must be non-scientific and non-logical avenues to truth. He can claim good logical grounds for rejecting the suggestion that there are two kinds of truth: the objective and the subjective. What is true is true, he may argue; what cannot be known cannot be known. Such truisms can be cited by the religious believer in support of his view that his beliefs have no special status in these respects, whether favourable or unfavourable.

The question remains undecided, then, on such general grounds as these, how far religion is similar to, how far dissimilar from, other areas of the curriculum. But epistemological considerations such as these suggest that for the sceptic all areas of the curriculum may be equally open to doubt, so that special scepticism in respect of religion is hard to justify. Kuhn has argued that even the paradigm of scientific knowledge itself is as shifting and unreliable in any absolute and permanent sense as are such traditionally disputable areas as morals and religion.[8] Mathematics offers a firmer standard, but it can be argued here, too, that its truths depend on the axioms and definitions employed. So without finally settling the wider theological debate, it is possible to claim with some justification that the area of religion is not unique in respect of its susceptibility to challenge, doubt, or scepticism. Science itself is based on assumptions which are not untimately amenable to proof. There can be no solution to the problem of justifying the inductive reasoning on which science is based, since even accepting the finality of disproof of a scientific law is to make the inductive assumption that what has failed to work once cannot be relied upon to work in the future. Science, it may be argued, requires fundamental acceptance of its distinctive methods, which cannot be based on any further external justification. Even the strong claims of logic can be subjected to a similar critique, since logic itself cannot be justified by any system external to it. Hence the idea that religious beliefs are totally different in their lack of external justification from the beliefs which feature in other curriculum areas is not incontrovertible. To argue, then, for a particular view of religious education on the basis of an analysis of religion which sets it apart from all other areas is to argue from an insecure basis.

It remains, though, to consider whether there are any special considerations which apply in the case of religious education which are not dependent on the epistemological status of religious belief, but which may nevertheless justify a distinctive approach with particular implications as far as state intervention and control are concerned.

The first point to be made is that, whatever may justifiably be claimed about its logical basis, as a matter of fact there is far more widespread disagreement on the matter of religious truth than there is about other types of truth, and political and social arrangements therefore need to be made which take account of that disagreement.

Secondly, it is not a matter of indifference to those who believe themselves to be in possession of religious truth whether others, and particularly the young, should come to accept it. For this reason schools which are religious foundations will, at least historically, have been based on what may be called the commitment position. Clearly, too, religious education holds the special place it has been assigned in some countries in the curriculum of schools and colleges on the assumption that it will be committed in nature and intent. These considerations explain to some extent the support for separate religious schools, the motivation for which is essentially twofold: first, the welfare of the young themselves, which is held to depend upon being brought up in the religion in question; and secondly, the maintenance of the religion, which is held to be dependent on uninterrupted generational transfer. But these considerations lead away from the examination of fundamental questions about the nature of religious education to the questions described earlier as consequent, and these will now need to be considered directly.

The position of those who favour religious schooling on the grounds just outlined can be challenged either by co-religionists who do not share these assumptions, or by those who are altogether opposed to the religion in question. As far as the first group are concerned, they are likely to argue that it is possible to hold a religion and also to believe that one's children may lead happy and fulfilled lives outside that religion. On the second point they may argue that a religion can survive independently of the family structure. Where the second group are concerned - the non-believers - they will of course deny both the connection of the religion with well-being and the importance of its survival. But whatever the validity of these arguments, some of which relate to matters of fact, others to matters of evaluation, they do not necessarily provide a reason for the legal exclusion of religious schooling contrary to the wishes of those who remain unconvinced by them. For this would be to assign to the state an ability to arbitrate between the divergent points of view which does not properly belong to it. On the contrary, the function of the state can only be to provide a conflict-free setting for the different viewpoints. Rather than attempt to settle the substantial issues, then, as far as legislation is concerned, the situation that leaves open the greatest number of possibilities is the one to be preferred.

It is important to consider how far the way in which its approach to this task will be affected by whether the state in question is a secular state or a religious state. In practice a secular state may be tolerant and a religious state intolerant, although from a purely theoretic point of view it might be expected that the secular state would be antithetical to religious education and a religious state sympathetic to alternative forms of religious expression.

Where the Christian religion is concerned, the differing role assigned to religious education in Britain and the USA conforms to some extent to theoretic expectations. The former, in spite of objections by some free-thinkers, is constitutionally regarded as a Christian state, while the latter, although containing at least as widespread support for Christianity as exists in Britain, has - originally for religious reasons - its status as a secular state jealously guarded and maintained. In Britain, then, the position of denominational schools is safeguarded, and religious education has the distinction of being the only compulsory subject on the timetable of state-funded schools, although the right of parents to withdraw their children from such education is equally carefully protected. The content of the education provided is itself drawn up in the Agreed Syllabus which ended self-damaging interdenominational conflict in the late nineteenth century. By contrast, American schools must avoid any religious ceremonial including the use of prayers, and are under pressure to exclude any kind of activity having reference to major religious festivals such as Christmas or Easter. Thus nativity plays, carol-singing and similar traditional activities are increasingly seen as having no place in the education which the secular state should provide. In France, as a further contrast, the solution has been the release of children on an agreed afternoon for parentally arranged religious education.

Two separate questions can be identified in contemplating the range and variety of practices and in attempting to seek sound principles on which to base decisions: the first concerns the role of the state in relation to the existence of religious or denominational schools financed and supported by independent effort; the second concerns the role of the state in relation to the provision of religious education within a state system of education.

It may seem that the first of these questions has a more obvious answer in the case of a state at least nominally committed to a particular religion, and indeed it may well be easy to settle without controversy the commitment of a Christian state to the existence of various forms of Christian schooling, although differences between Christian denominations may be as keenly felt as differences between religions. The relation of a nominally Christian state to non-Christian religious schools, however, raises more readily recognisable problems, similar to those identifiable in a Jewish state, or a Hindu state, or a new Islamic state, with regard to schools of different faiths within their boundaries. In the light of these problems, it is important to see what arguments might be advanced for the proscribing of schools of an alien faith, and might prevent those who advocate such a course from seeing it as an act of repression and intolerance.

Essentially, what might be put forward is an argument in terms of rationality and consistency. From the point of view of the committed state the toleration of alien religious schooling is the toleration of error and falsehood. Moreover, if education is seen as the propagation of truth, then alien religious education will appear as a denial of education. A similar problem may arise in the case of a secular state. States may maintain their secularity either because they hold religion to be a matter for the individual rather than the state or, as in the case of Marxist states, because they reject religion altogether on behalf of their citizens. While the first position does avoid the problem of apparent inconsistency, in the latter case the secular state which permits religious schooling may again appear to be involved in contradiction in permitting to flourish that which it wholly denies.

But the apparent irrationality on the part of the state which is involved in the endorsing of contradictory positions derives from an illegitimate anthropomorphising of the state. An individual, if he believes A to be true, must believe not-A to be false; but it has already been suggested that the function of the state, unlike the individual, is not to eliminate inconsistent beliefs but to reconcile contradictory viewpoints, or at least to defuse them and ensure that they will not be causes of conflict and danger to the individuals within its boundaries. Hence a state whose function is conceived of in this limited light, whether committed to a particular religious viewpoint or not, must adopt a standpoint of religious toleration.

In the previous chapter it was suggested that freedom of religion and freedom of religious schooling do, as a matter of fact, go hand in hand. If this is so, then the state, whether religious or secular, in adopting a position of religious toleration commits itself also to permitting the existence of religious educational establishments, even where it is unsympathetic to the religion in question. Two qualifications need to be set to this, however. If a religion is, in a political sense, itself repressive, then the state's obligation to protect individual freedom must in this case express itself in a ban on the recruitment of minors to that religion through special schooling. It is a matter of controversy which sects this qualification would exclude, but the 1978 Jonestown slaughter in Guyana is an extreme example in which few would deny the principle that children may need to be protected from being coerced into sharing the beliefs and practices of their elders. Secondly, special circumstances, such as those at present applying in Northern Ireland, may also justify a different approach to the question of denominational schooling. In this case one principle that might be applied is that of whether a religious grouping has become identified with a political or revolutionary movement. What these qualifications amount to, then, is that a state which is committed to non-intervention on religious grounds may in special cases need to intervene on grounds which belong to its proper sphere of interest - the protection of individuals or the preservation of peace and political stability.

Nevertheless, recognising these qualifications should not obscure the realisation that toleration is essentially a matter of accepting what on all other grounds would be rejected. The question of toleration does not arise in the case of what is supported or agreed with. The fact that a state is committed to a particular religion, then, or to no religion at all, cannot justify its suppression of an alien faith. It follows that the attitude of a state to religious education will be a strong indicator of its character either as a totalitarian state seeking to dominate and control the lives of its citizens, or as a liberal state dedicated to the principles of freedom and toleration.

The liberal state, must, then, by its very nature, permit the existence of religious schools, while recognising that their approach to religious education is bound to be a committed one. Where the common resources of the community are providing schooling, though, some difference of approach is justifiable. There can be no more case for excluding religious education altogether from the timetable than for excluding any of the other major areas of human thought. But the degree of commitment involved on the part of the teacher, and the degree of commitment to be sought from the student, will depend to a considerable extent on the general view taken of impartiality and indoctrination in teaching. This question will be more fully discussed in the next chapter, but if in the case of religious education a more impartial, information-giving approach is favoured, the problem of reconciling the conflicting interests of student, teacher, parent, religious bodies and society in general is more easily resolved. As long as there is some broad agreement that in principle religion is on par with other subjects, and that it is the facts of human nature rather than of its own logical structure which mark it out for special attention, then answers to the practical questions relating to state-provided education may leave room for compromise. Some indication of the lines of such a compromise may, however, be given.

First, the state must not be found to be in the position of enforcing belief or unbelief, since this is incompatible with its role of religious toleration. Secondly, however, since religion is an important aspect of the culture and tradition of a society, the individuals who make up the state, and in particular individual parents, may reasonably demand that institutional arrangements are made which will favour the continuity of that tradition and culture, and make a positive contribution to the upbringing of children within the religion of their parents. This, however, has implications for the teacher who undertakes such a task. From this point of view, the most widely acceptable solution is that the approach to teaching employed should be one which respects the autonomy or later mature independent judgement of the student. So long as this requirement is met, the teacher may himself be committed or uncommitted, believer or unbeliever, and may be disposed to, or indifferent to, the generation of belief in the students he teaches. This position has the advantage of being acceptable also to those members of the society who do not share its majority religion or who may not wish their children to be influenced towards it.

Such an approach to teaching cannot be described solely in the context of religious education, for the notions of indoctrination, impartiality and neutrality which are implicit here have a wider role to play in other areas of education. The solution that is being suggested here can, then, only be fully understood within the framework of this wider conception of indoctrination, which must now be considered independently.

NOTES: CHAPTER 5

1   DES, *Children and their Primary Schools,* a report of the Central Advisory Council for Education (London: HMSO, 1966), Vol. 1.
2   R. Marples, 'Is religious education possible?', *Journal of Philosophy of Education,* vol. 12 (1978), pp. 81-91.
3   W. D. Hudson, 'Is religious education possible?', in G. Langford and D. J. O'Connor (eds), *New Essays in Philosophy of Education* (London: Routledge & Kegan Paul, 1973), p. 176.
4   J. Sealey, 'Education as a second-order form of experience and its relation to religion', *Journal of Philosophy of Education,* vol. 13 (1979), pp. 83-90.
5   P. Hirst, *Modern Education in a Secular Society* (London: University of London Press, 1974), p. 84.
6   ibid., p. 82.
7   ibid., p. 86.
8   T. Kuhn, *The Structure of Scientific Revolutions* (Chicago: University of Chicago Press, 1970).

Chapter 6

Morality, Politics and Indoctrination

Both historical and etymological considerations suggest a link between the topic of the last chapter, religious education, and the topic of indoctrination. In the early stages of the long evolution to a modern educational system education was identified with religious education, and, as Gatchel has shown in his account of the evolution of the concept of indoctrination,[1] in the Middle Ages religious education was equated with indoctrination in the strict sense of the passing on of the doctrines - literally, teachings - of the Roman Catholic Church. Hence the preceding discussion of the scope and place of religious education is especially pertinent to the question of indoctrination, although in contemporary discussions this is seen as a wider problem relevant possibly to all teaching areas, but with special implications for the teaching of morals and politics as well as religion.

Morals and politics are two areas where the interests of the individual - his right and aspiration to self-determination - are especially vulnerable to both the organised control of the state and the informal interference of society through social pressure and influence. In education, state and society have a tool which can, if the will is present, be employed with powerful effect in securing conformity and compliance by damping down incipient embers of disagreement or criticism at an early stage, before they can flare up into non-conformity or revolution. Such an approach to education is what many would understand by the term indoctrination today, and a common expectation would be that it would accurately describe the situation in many totalitarian countries.

There is a deeper interpretation of the notion, however, which sees indoctrination as something of a more subtle nature altogether, capable of posing a threat within a liberal society and even within a system of schooling not consciously or intentionally directed to the dogmatic moulding of opinion. Within this conception of in-doctrination, discussion has tended to focus on the search for a principle for demarcating indoctrinatory and non-indoctrinatory processes in typical teaching situations. Such principles might centre on the subject-matter under discussion, or on the actual methods employed, or on the aims and intentions of the teacher.

As far as the first of these criteria is concerned, the argument of the previous chapter in respect of religion demonstrated the difficulty of making an epistemological distinction between subjects in respect of their certainty and rationality, or their association with public and objective standards of verification. Nevertheless, both John Wilson[2] and R. F. Atkinson[3] have defended the view that indoctrination can best be understood as teaching as fact what is in reality a matter of opinion. Where this view is accepted, morals, religion and politics will tend to be located in the realm of opinion, and standard curriculum subjects in the realm of fact. Such a division, however, in spite of its initial plausibility, does not stand up to close examination. The study of literature for example, involves questions of taste; the study of history involves selection of facts and data together with arbitration on what is relevant and irrelevant; science reflects the preoccupations of the scientists of our place and era; and mathematics, as has already been emphasised, is a system which follows only from the assumptions which we care to make; and, indeed, young children today are trained to vary those assumptions and thus reach conclusions which are very different from those which strike an individual for whom, for example, arithmetic on a decimal base is the assumed standard.

But again, the point that became clear in the case of religion turns out to have a more general relevance here. While the basis for making an epistemological distinction between subjects is challengeable, philosophical scepticism being a broom with a tendency to sweep all before it, there is an undeniable practical distinction to be recognised between matters about which people as a matter of fact disagree strongly, and matters of consensus. But while this distinction suggests the need for compromise and negotiation where actual teaching programmes are concerned, it is not clear that it is strong enough to function as a criterion of indoctrination. It needs to be borne in mind, too, that other factors may operate to make the differences between religion, politics and morals as significant as the differences between this group of subjects and others.

It will be important to return to this point, but first some consideration must be given to those suggested criteria which do not depend on the nature of the subject-matter. In one of the earliest contemporary discussions of the nature of indoctrination R. M. Hare argues that the difference between indoctrination and morally acceptable education lies in the intention of the educator. The indoctrinator, argues Hare, looks for signs of independence of thought in his students only to suppress them; his aim is to keep his students as perpetual children. The educator, on the other hand, welcomes such attitudes as the signs of maturity - indications that the adolescents in his charge are becoming adults.[4] Others have proposed a similar criterion in more specific terms. It was suggested by John White, for example, that an indoctrinator's aim is to instil the belief that *p* (where *p* may stand for any proposition at all) in such a way that nothing will shake that belief.[5] Ivan Snook, who criticises White for not dealing adequately with the problem of whether the notion of indoctrination can be held to apply where *p* may be true rather than a false or questionable proposition, himself proposes that a person is indoctrinating if (1) in his teaching he is actively desiring that pupils believe what he is teaching regardless of the evidence, or (2) he foresees that as a result of his teaching such an outcome is likely or inevitable.[6]

A more general but useful definition offered by Snook in summary is this:

> Indoctrination implies a pejorative judgment on a teaching situation. It suggests that someone is taking advantage of a privileged role to influence those under his charge in a manner which is likely to distort their ability to assess the evidence on its own merit. The positive intention to bring about this state of mind is sufficient.[7]

Whilst Snook's position has much to recommend it, it has to be recognised that positive intention is itself a state of mind. And as long as indoctrination is used in the pejorative sense just described - a sense which is commonly assumed in English usage of the present day - such an intangible criterion as a state of mind is, without further explanation, an inadequate tool with which to solve the overt and practical problem of recognising indoctrination within an educational system.

For this reason, if the intention criterion were to be retained, it would be necessary to support the notion of intention with some description of the ways in which the intention to indoctrinate could be recognised. These modes of recognition would then become, in practical terms, descriptions of methods of teaching, reached by observation of teaching and learning situations. Indeed, the point was once expressed by the present writer in the following terms:

> The teacher of bias, the teacher who, whatever his protestations, is concerned to indoctrinate, can be identified whenever one of a number of points of view is presented as though it were the only

one possible; whenever questions are suppressed rather than answered; whenever certain areas of questioning are taboo; and whenever the educator is psychologically unable to tolerate the expression of dissenting views.[8]

While these tests were proposed as a measure of indoctrinatory intention, it is arguable that, since they do in fact describe a method of teaching, method alone might better be regarded as the central criterion of indoctrination. There are some practical considerations which might count against this. For instance, indoctrinatory methods would commonly not be understood in the above sense, but rather as a reference to practices of a much more crude and overt nature - those described by Sargant, for example, in *Battle for the Mind,* which consist in gross brainwashing practices, involving possibly torture, solitary confinement, use of drugs, sensory deprivation, semi-starvation, or deprivation of sleep; or perhaps straightforward propaganda, or subliminal advertising.[9] These methods are very easy to recognise, and as long as they play no part in the educational practices of a society it may be argued that emphasis on method as a criterion of indoctrination may lull its members into a false sense of security as regards the absence of indoctrination. Moreover, as long as such practices occur in some societies it may seem a devaluation of the notion of indoctrination to equate it with the more subtle methods earlier described. Nevertheless, the inference to be drawn from these objections is in fact precisely the reverse of what the objectors suggest; indeed, the more free a society is from the cruder indoctrinatory practices, the more important becomes recognition of the more subtle ways in which indoctrination can manifest itself.

A further argument against accepting method *tout court* as the standard of indoctrination is advanced by Snook, who suggests that certain methods are grounds for moral objection only in the case of controversial subject-matter. Therefore, he suggests, method alone is insufficient as a criterion and must be combined with the criterion of content. And even when this is done, in certain cases, such as the moral training of very young children, apparently indoctrinatory, non-rational methods are both necessary and justified. He argues that, particularly in the last case, it is the absence of indoctrinatory intention that makes such practices acceptable. But this suggestion gives rise to a problem about unacknowledged or even unconscious intention. If behavioural tests such as the ones described above are applied in judging intention, then an observer could judge that an intention to indoctrinate existed when the teacher concerned was unaware of it and even denied it. For this reason, and also because most indoctrinators do not acknowledge an intention to indoctrinate, it seems preferable to regard the behavioural tests proposed as applying to the methods employed rather than indirectly, to the intention of the teacher. If Snook is right and these methods are in fact necessary where very young children are concerned, or harmless in the case of certain subject-matter, then it may be preferable to concede that there is an area where indoctrination is acceptable, rather than to adopt the notion of unconscious intention.

One of the behavioural tests mentioned involved reference to informing students of the variety of viewpoints possible on a particular issue. The notion that all such viewpoints (subject only to the conditions of relevance and importance) should be presented is essentially what is implied by the notion of impartiality. Sometimes no distinction is made between this notion and that of neutrality. But while the avoidance of indoctrination does require impartiality, it does not necessarily involve neutrality. Contrary to the purely verbal implication, it is possible to be partial (i.e. personally committed to a particular viewpoint) and also impartial, in the sense of dealing fairly with alternative viewpoints. What is not possible is to be committed and neutral at the same time on the same subject. Impartiality should not, therefore, be equated with neutrality, and it is perfectly possible to favour the first and not the second.

Applying this distinction within the three controversial areas of religion, morals and politics, some practical differences become clear. If religion is in question, a believer cannot - by definition - be neutral. He can, however, display impartiality in familiarising his students with other systems of belief, possibly concealing his own commitment. But there would be considerable disagreement as to the desirability or moral necessity of this latter strategy. It would in any case be unlikely that his own belief could remain hidden from his students, if only because of the demands made by most religions in terms of physical participation in formalised ritual, usually involving public attendance at a place of worship.

Where morality is in question the commitment of the teacher to a particular viewpoint is arguably required by the nature of his profession, since he is constantly confronted with situations in which he is obliged to sanction certain types of behaviour and oppose others. Moreover, the ideal of neutrality can be resisted here by strong arguments about the nature of morality, the essential force of these arguments being that to employ moral language is in itself to commit oneself to a particular moral point of view.[10] Neutrality in this case is only likely to be recommended in cases where a genuine agnosticism about what is right or wrong already exists on the part of the teacher.

This explains why it has been recommended as a strategy for moral education particularly where matters of sexual morals are concerned, since this is an area where genuine uncertainty often exists, while the weakness of the approach has tended to manifest itself on racial issues, where the teacher is less likely to feel that alternative moral positions to his own may be justified.[11]

Politics, however, at least in two- or multi-party democracies, is built on the notion that alternative positions are to be allowed to flourish. The politician of an opposition party is not usually regarded by his government opponents in the same way as an atheist is regarded by a theist - as being fundamentally and dangerously wrong. Nor does a view that a particular strategy should be adopted necessarily entail that other strategies must be wrong, in the way that a moral conviction that murder is wrong entails that those who favour it are morally mistaken. In a democracy, in other words, political issues are open in a way in which religious and moral issues, for the individual, are not.

This view of politics has been challlenged by Grenville Wall in a discussion of the special problems of political education.[12] Wall identifies two particular dilemmas for political education: the first is the problem of the apparent inconsistency of 'dogmatic liberalism', which is defined as teaching traditional liberal principles concerning freedom of the individual; encouraging a disposition to observe these principles in practice; and instructing students in the use of liberal-democratic institutions and processes. The problem Wall sees here is that some would argue that to teach this as the 'right' or 'only' political approach is as much of a violation of the principles of freedom it professes as is political indoctrination in a Marxist state.

The second problem identified by Wall is that of the danger, where most education is state education, of the state coming to exercise an improper influence over opinion. As a possible solution to the first and possibly also the second of these difficulties, Wall considers J. S. Mill's proposal that teaching and examining should be restricted to facts, not values. The application of this distinction within the curriculum has already been questioned here, and Wall also rejects it, both on the ground that the fact-value distinction is itself disputable and also because he considers that values actually play an important part in political education. He argues that it is Mill's ultimate scepticism (or at least subjectivism) about values that provides the ultimate rationale of his liberalism. Wall therefore turns instead to consideration of the view that values themselves can be divided into those which are substantive and those which are procedural, and that while the first may be part and parcel of a particular political system, the second may be compatible with many political and social systems, so that to adopt them is not to be in any sense partisan. This view is an essential element in Bernard Crick's claim that the aim of political education can and should be 'political literacy'.[13] The procedural values identified by Crick are freedom, toleration, fairness, respect for truth and respect for reasoning, and he claims that these are essentially educational values in being both rational and public. As substantive values, on the other hand, he cites equality, justice when used to justify authority, and the values embodied in religious, ethical and political doctrines.

Indoctrination, then, on Crick's view, will only occur when the procedural values he has described are ignored, and it cannot be identified with insisting on these procedural values as part of political education. It is Wall's view, however, that a sound approach to political education cannot be built on the foundation of this distinction between procedural and substantive values, for substantive values are essentially no more open than procedural ones. It is not the case, Wall argues, that there may be two or more 'correct' but contradictory beliefs, since this is to exclude the possibility of rational decisions being made on matters of politics. There must, on the contrary, he argues, be rational criteria for the selection of goals of political action.

Essentially, Wall is arguing, as R. M. Hare does on matters of moral language, for the universalisability of decisions of political principle. But politics is founded on the existence of special interests, for unanimity of opinion and coincidence of interest would make politics unnecessary. Moreover, who a person is makes a great deal of difference to what, politically, that person wants. Morality, by contrast, appeals to what is universal in man's existence, and in a quite different sense transcends time, place and culture. The idea that there are 'correct' beliefs in politics, then - beliefs which would be shared by any rational person - cannot be used to refute the 'political literacy' approach to political education, nor to reinforce dogmatic approaches to the teaching of politics. Nevertheless, it is arguable that the dichotomy of political values on which the 'political literacy' approach is based is ultimately unjustifiable, not, as Wall argues because substantive values are as closed as procedural ones, but rather because procedural values are as much the subject of choice and commitment as substantive ones. If this is so, then the very possibility, or conceivability, of a genuinely open and uncommitted form of political education must be seriously in question.

What is not in question, however, is that many people interested in political education in fact reject such a notion even as an ideal to be aimed at. Anthony Arblaster, for example, describes an ideal of such education in which teaching would be in the hands of people actively committed to and professing different political viewpoints.[14] Marcuse proposes that the liberal or conventional concept of tolerance as extending equally to all views, whether of the right or of the left, should be replaced by the radical concept of 'liberating tolerance' which is defined as 'intolerance against movements from the Right and toleration of movements from the Left'.[15] Many of the university 'free speech' confrontations in the 1970s employed such an ideology - an ideology in terms of which the defender of politically committed education is happy to use liberal arguments to secure himself a place and a hearing, but having secured them, to use his position for the stifling of any point of view in conflict with his own - most conspicuously, of course, of views at the opposite end of the political spectrum to his own. Given these open confessions of policy, then, it is clear that for liberals political education could turn out to be the Trojan horse of totalitarianism and intolerance.

At this point it may be useful to sum up the practical conclusions which it is being suggested here are entailed by what has so far been said concerning the possibility of indoctrination in religious, moral and political education. The question of religious education was considered in the last chapter, and there it was argued that religious freedom is best protected by a combination of independently supported religious schools, and an approach to religious education in state schools which is non-indoctrinatory but not necessarily non-committed, impartiality rather than neutrality being the appropriate aim. The further considerations of the nature of indoctrination that have been reviewed here have supported this view. Where moral education is concerned, an individual's right to his own moral life can only be exercised on the basis of an early understanding of the essentially committed character of morality, and the impossibility of moral neutrality as a generalised approach to matters of moral principle. However, the individual's right to his own political viewpoint is best safeguarded in the light of what we know about human nature and about some declared politically committed positions by the absence of political teaching in schools. The notion of schools established to reflect a particular political viewpoint (parallel to denominational religious schools) is clearly anathema in a democratic context, so that unlike the issue of religion, the issue of politics relates only to what is provided within the established educational system and any ground-rules aimed at will have general applicability. Within this framework parents may rightly object to attempts to win their children over to a particular point of view.

Finally, the question may be raised of whether there are any other ways, other than direct political teaching, in which the education system may conceal an indoctrinatory threat? Some would argue that such a threat might lie in state control of the ordinary curriculum. However, France is a country which has long had rigid centralised control of the curriculum without charges of indoctrination being levied; while it is in the United States, which has no centralised control of education, that problems of indoctrination have been raised from time to time in, for example, such matters as the teaching of evolutionary theory. In Britain, where very considerable freedom in respect of the curriculum has remained in the hands of teachers, the problem of curriculum control is seen as essentially one of negotiation, and the state, if it is seen as playing a part at all, may be seen in the role of adjudicator between the interested parties: teachers, parents and the children themselves with their practical and vocational needs.

While, therefore, it would be wrong to see the state's interest in the curriculum as inevitably linked to indoctrination, it is clear that there may exist a dangerous ambiguity in its role. State intervention will appear in a favourable light when it arises, for example, in those rare cases where a headteacher chooses to exercise despotic powers against the advice of his colleagues and in defiance of parental opinion. A better solution in these cases would, however, be reached by the negotiation of a more equitable balance of power between all concerned, including, in the later stages of education, the reasoned preferences of students, and by ensuring, as was argued earlier, that state education is not the only education available. But teaching is a personal relationship, and whilst attention to the macro-structure is important, the essence of indoctrination lies in the personal level where teacher and taught meet in a relationship which is characterised either by its openness, or by its closed nature.

Finally, the danger of indoctrination might be said to lie not in the teaching of the acknowledged and agreed curriculum of the school but in what has been called the 'hidden curriculum'. De-schoolers, including such writers as Ivan Illich and Everitt Reimer, would argue that schools actually pass on very successfully the values and system of the society in which they exist. 'This hidden curriculum', Illich writes, 'serves as a ritual of initiation into a growth-oriented consumer society for rich and poor alike.'[16] Others have argued that it is the child's social class position and occupational expectations that are being tacitly conveyed by the education system. Sociological analyses of what teachers actually say and do when, for example, *intending* to teach mathematics, can be very illuminating and in fact support the notion of unintentional indoctrination which has been proposed here.

However, it is important not to generalise from particular cases; nor to move from accepting that sometimes teachers form expectations concerning their students which then affect the students' own self-image, to the very different thesis that all education is indoctrination. It would be even less justifiable to generalise from the examples which focus on notions of social class (often with the acknowledged intention of supporting an orthodox Marxist thesis concerning social class and education rather than from a spirit of open inquiry) to a global view of the educational enterprise which finds indoctrination within a liberal society, and by implication assumes a contrast which plainly does not exist with non-capitalist social systems. In other words, the 'hidden curriculum' argument proves either too little or too much. Either it does succeed in unveiling small-scale indoctrinatory practices in particular situations - practices which would be conceded to be indoctrinatory according to the criteria set out in this chapter - without providing any ground for concluding that these practices are universal; or it suggests a notion of indoctrination which is so wide that virtually no education system and no society could avoid it. If indoctrination is seriously to be regarded as a threat, however, something more specific than this must be identified, and the threat guarded against, not only by appeal to better personal attitudes on the part of teachers, but more concretely, by ensuring that a variety of institutions exists, so that any kind of monopoly in education, but particularly that of the state, may be avoided.

NOTES: CHAPTER 6

1 R. H. Gatchel, 'The evolution of the concept', in I. Snook (ed.), *Concepts of Indoctrination* (London: Routledge & Kegan Paul, 1972), pp. 9-16.
2 J. Wilson, 'Education and indoctrination', in T. H. B. Hollins (ed.), *Aims in Education* (Manchester: Manchester University Press, 1964), pp. 24-46.
3 R. F. Atkinson, 'Instruction and indoctrination', in R. D. Archambault (ed.), *Philosophical Analysis and Education* (London: Routledge & Kegan Paul, 1965), pp. 171-86;
4 R. M. Hare, 'Adolescents into adults', in T. H. B. Hollins (ed.), *Aims in Education* (Manchester: Manchester University Press, 1964), pp. 47-70.
5 J. P. White, 'Indoctrination', in R. S. Peters (ed.), *The Concept of Education* (London: Routledge & Kegan Paul, 1967), pp. 177-91.
6 I. Snook, *Indoctrination and Education* (London: Routledge & Kegan Paul, 1972), p. 50.
7 ibid., p. 66.
8 B. Cohen, 'Bias and indoctrination', in D. Heater (ed.), *The Teaching of Politics* (London: Methuen, 1969), p. 180.
9 W. Sargant, *Battle for the Mind* (London: Pan, 1963).
10 Some of these arguments are presented in B. Cohen, 'Principles and situations - the

liberal dilemma and moral education', *Proceedings of the Aristotelian Society,* vol. LXXVI (1975).

11   These differences have been illustrated in the United Kingdom in the use of the Humanities Curriculum Project teaching packs on these topics, which were based on the neutralist ideal. The project, sponsored by the Schools Council and the Nuffield Foundation, was set up in 1967 under the directorship of Lawrence Stenhouse.

12   G. Wall, 'Political literacy and the liberal theory of political education', Paper delivered at the Annual Conference of the Philosophy of Education Society of Great Britain at the Froebel Institute, London, 4 January 1980.

13   B. Crick and A. Porter, *Political Education and Political Literacy* (London: Longman, 1978).

14   A. Arblaster, 'Education and ideology', in D. Rubenstein and C. Stoneman (eds), *Education for Democracy* (Harmondsworth: Penguin, 1970), pp. 53-4.

15   H. Marcuse, 'Repressive tolerance' in R. P. Wolff *et al.*, *A Critique of Pure Tolerance* (London: Cape, 1969), pp. 122-3.

16   I. Illich, *De-Schooling Society* (London: Calder & Boyars, 1971), p. 33.

Chapter 7

The Ideological Background: Mill or Marx?

The underlying theme of the discussion so far has been the conflict in various areas of education between the demands or wishes of the individual and the claims of the state. It is now time to bring this fundamental problem to the surface and to attempt to uncover the basic ideological conflict which is its source. Ultimately, of course, compromise is required between the pressing claims of state and individual: complete individual freedom is anarchy and, as such, self-defeating, since no individual - even the strongest, as Hobbes pointed out - can enjoy freedom without the security provided by a framework of law; similarly, but less commonly recognised, even absolute state power involves the freedom of individuals at the top of the hierarchy or bureaucracy to impose their conception of what the state requires. But within these limits, which illustrate the inherently contradictory nature of the notions of either total individual freedom or total state control, the difference between those who would prefer to see the balance of decision-making power in the hands of the individual and those who would prefer to see it in the hands of the state is of crucial significance, nowhere more so than in the area of education. But since education is primarily concerned with the young and politically impotent, and since even without the additional factor of youth the individual wields little power against the organised might of the state, the contrast in the special case of education must be drawn in terms of the family rather than the individual. Subject to this qualification, however, it may be said that the ideological difference in question can be explained in terms of two traditions in political thought, which are represented by the continuing influence of the two thinkers who, in popular understanding, represent these contrasting viewpoints: John Stuart Mill and Karl Marx.

One significant date coincidentally confirms this juxtaposition. In 1859 Mill published his essay *On Liberty,* an essay which stands as a continuing argument for the claims of the individual against the state, and for the limitation of state interference in personal life to the minimum necessary for the prevention of harm. In the same year, Karl Marx published his *A Contribution to the Critique of Political*

Economy, a work which is based on a view of society and of world history in which the contribution of individual will and choice is made totally subservient to and dependent upon material and economic factors over which the individual has no control. The present-day contrast, then, can be seen as between those - usually called liberals and democrats - whose ideological roots lie in Mill's conception of freedom as non-interference, and those whose ideological stance is conditioned by the Marxist analysis of society as something divisible not into the atoms of individuals or individual families, but into the subgroups of social class and economic stratification.

This distinction should not be confused with another and perhaps more obvious ideological contrast - that between the political left and the political right. For the liberal/totalitarian contrast cuts across the left/right categorisation. Political ideologies of both left and right may denigrate individual freedom and self-determination - fascism, for example, personifies and reifies the state - while freedom is far from being a right-wing interest. In education, however, these contrasts have become blurred, and left-wing ideologies in particular have shown an anti-individualist bias, while claims for freedom from state direction, particularly where independent schools are concerned, have become associated with the political right. However, the existence of an essentially left-wing de-schooling movement casts doubt on this prevailing categorisation, and suggests a potential community of interests in the case of educational freedom for those who sympathies lie with either political left or political right. An antithesis based simply on drawing a line between left and right should therefore be resisted, both in the interest of education and also in the interest of the wider society. More important in both these respects is the antithesis symbolised in the contrast between Mill and Marx.

It should be said, in embarking on such a contrast, that Mill and Marx, in their extensive writings on a multitude of subjects, shared sometimes surprising similarities. Both, for example, had a view of education which excluded religion, and both a conception of morality which derived from human need rather than divine revelation. Sometimes, too, each individually advocates something which seems strictly incompatible with the overall position he propounds - as when, for instance, Mill remarks that the state may be fully justified in interfering in the freedom to marry and procreate, or when Marx manifests his moral disapproval of the excesses of the capitalist system. Nevertheless, irrespective of such qualifications, it is Mill as the defender of the liberal values of freedom, privacy, autonomy and self-determination who provides the contrast in question here; while it is the Marx whose ideas have inspired contemporary collectivist societies and movements who stands as the contrast to him, rather than the Marx who, historically and personally, may well have valued individualism, and whose system ultimately involved the natural dissolution of the apparatus of the state.

Even within these limits, however, it is necessary to note two further points of agreement between the two thinkers. In putting forward the doctrine of economic determination, Marx pointed out that before men can pursue politics, art or religion they must first satisfy the needs of their human nature. These, however, he saw as essentially material - the need to eat and drink and be sheltered from the elements. Mill, in a very comparable turn of phrase, said 'Men are men before they are lawyers or physicians or merchants or manufacturers',[1] although the prior need to which Mill was pointing was more directly educational - a need for a liberal (i.e. non-vocational) education.

Secondly, both Mill and Marx could be said to hold a similar view regarding the long-term or ultimate dispensability of the state. For Mill anything other than the minimal state was an intrusion into the liberty of the individual. In a well-known paragraph he urged that 'the sole end for which mankind is warranted, individually or collectively, in interfering with the liberty of action of any of their number, is self-protection' and 'the only part of the conduct of anyone, for which he is amenable to society, is that which concerns others . . . Over himself, over his own mind and body, the individual is sovereign.'[2] The ideal implied here is one involving a minimum of legislative interference, but also one according to which a society of equal and well-disposed men would scarcely be aware of the state, which would need to be retained as an organisation only for the sake of the anti-social or the psychotic, who could rightly be restrained. When comparison is made with the notion of an ultimate developed communist society, a very similar ideal of the state finally 'withering away' is to be found - a suggestion which carries the implication that the organised state is required only where the interests of individuals conflict and run counter to each other, and that such conflict is unnatural under ideal conditions.

The contrast to be drawn here, then, is set within the boundaries of an agreement that the so-called 'higher' and more complex pursuits of man, and particularly the cultural and political aspects which are of most significance educationally, are secondary to the common needs of man simply as a human being, whether, as in the Marxist case these common needs are seen as confined to the basic material level, or whether, as Mill assumed, a minimal broad educational requirement is added. Secondly, the ultimate dispensability of the state is seen as a consequence of an idealised human nature.

This second point, however, carries very different implications in the two cases. Mill's liberalism is not utopian and some state interference may be presumed to be necessary in all forms of society, so that no foreseeable end will be set to the need to monitor closely the limits of that interference. The Marxist position, however, in assuming an ultimate coincidence of interests once class conflict is abolished, removes also the need for restraints on the power of the state in a realised communist society. At the same time the need for such restraints at any earlier stage is simply irrelevant to the struggle to achieve the classless society. Mill did at times imply that fully rational and educated human nature might produce consensus on matters of political and moral controversy, but for the forms of society that he could foresee the possibility of a 'tyranny of the majority' over-shadowed such potential agreement and justified in his view a permanent vigilance in the protection of a plurality of viewpoints and their expression. For Marx, on the other hand, conflict and disagreement were temporary defects of only the split and transitional forms of society leading to communism. In the classless society he predicted that 'there will be no more political power properly so called, since political power is precisely the expression of antagonism in civil society'.[3] His view of human nature, then, is sanguine and optimistic: the end of poverty will bring the end of crime, the end of classes, the end of jealousy and strife. A natural harmony will be the characteristic of an ideal communist society based, essentially, on the natural suitability of man's nature for such a society.

It is interesting in this respect to compare Marx with Rousseau, for whom a similar optimism about the nature of man not only provided the blue-print for a theory of politics and society, but also supplied the starting-point for a theory of progressive education. 'God', wrote Rousseau, 'makes all things good, man meddles with them and they become evil.'[4] This led Rousseau to postulate non-interference as the guiding principle of education, and progressive educationists have followed him since in both the practical consequences which he inferred and in his starting-assumption concerning human nature, the natural goodness of the child. But while both Marx and Mill had specific views on education, they did not develop them as extensively as did Rousseau, and it is not their educational views that form the basis of the present contrast, but rather their fundamental social and political outlook.

It may be in some respects misleading to describe Marx's belief in the ultimate possibility of men living together without the repressive control of police or army as a theory of human nature, for Marx was emphatic in rejecting the idea of human nature in the abstract. This was because his materialistic account of the factors controlling human behaviour ruled out any continuing view of a basic human nature independent of social and cultural context. The economic form of Marx's materialism is well known, but its dialectical nature distinguishes it from more common forms of philosophical materialism. The dialectical aspect of Marx's theory was inspired by Hegel's dialectical system, although Marx claimed to have inverted Hegel's system in order to expose the rational kernel in its mystical shell.

Hegel's dialectic involved a progression of categories leading ultimately to what he termed the Absolute, through a process by which each category (thesis) evoked its opposite (antithesis), and the opposition thus produced evoked a synthesis which would itself produce a new opposition. Hegel himself applied this system to the process of history, but in his system the state was idealised, so that his account of history tended to lead to nationalism and ultimately to fascism. Marx, whilst regarding the idea of dialectical change as fruitful, substituted a dynamic account of historical change, in which the sequence of categories was from primitive communities through slave systems, then feudalism, to capitalism and ultimately socialism. Where Hegel had seen national or racial groups as the forces at work in the dialectical development, Marx considered that classes were the significant groups - that the force behind the dialectic of history was not the struggle of nations, but of classes.

Because the process of the dialectic was seen as historically inevitable, social laws being accorded comparable status to scientific laws, it is essentially deterministic. The determinism involved, however, is specifically materialistic. In applying this materialism to history, production is seen as the key factor in human life; and changes in the mode of production are held to produce social change. Productive forces and productive relations form the base of a pyramid on which is built a superstructure of religion, morals, law and government, mediated by arrangements for the holding of property. It is this phenomenon which produces the class struggle: Marx saw the significant division in society as being that between those who control the means of production, and those who do not. The national interest is therefore always the interest of the ruling class, and the causes of war are found to be economic rather than ideological. At the same time the role of great men in history has to be reinterpreted and reversed. Instead of saying that Napoleon changed the course of history, it is necessary to say that history created the conditions for the inevitable appearance of a Napoleon.

Morality, religion and law become linked with the interest of the dominant class, so that the objectivity of both ethical conduct and knowledge itself are ruled out, thus necessitating the relativistic morality and epistemology of present-day neo-Marxists and sympathisers. Within the field of education in particular these are characterised by the view that both forms of knowledge and also ethical values are socio-historical constructs embedded in the framework of a particular time and social system, and representing the interests of the dominant class.[5]

In contrast to this, Mill had a conception of truth as something capable of surviving the vicissitudes of history and the flotsam of social movements. He had, too, a secure valuation of certain principles - of justice, freedom and toleration, for example - which, again over the course of the fluctuations of human history and development, had been found to be in the long-term interest of the human race - in his phrase, 'grounded on the permanent interests of man as a progressive being'.[6] This not always recognised aspect of his thought is made clear in the fifth and final chapter of *Utilitarianism,* where he argues that the principle of justice has an over-riding importance even if its ultimate justification does lie in utility. He writes:

> While I dispute the pretensions of any theory which sets up an imaginary standard of justice not grounded on utility, I account the justice which is grounded on utility to be the chief part, and incomparably the most sacred and binding part, of all morality. Justice is a name for certain classes of moral rules, which concern the essentials of human well-being more nearly, and are therefore of more absolute obligation, than any other rules for the guidance of life.[7]

In *On Liberty* Mill defends the principles of freedom and toleration and displays an attitude to truth which makes one suspect that whatever his intellectual position as Bentham's successor and heir to the utilitarian doctrine these are values which he would hardly be prepared to sacrifice even if, as he believed not to be the case, they could be shown to be incompatible with utilitarian calculation. Where Mill's general social views are concerned, he claimed to have found inspiration for these in his reading of de Toqueville's *Democracy in America*, a book which emphasises the sacrifices of freedom which are necessitated by the pursuit of equality.

The possibility that a democratic majority might become as dangerous a tyrant as an individual dictator was a major inspiration of his defence of toleration and individual freedom. In *On Liberty,* therefore, he presents arguments for freedom of thought, freedom of expression, freedom of association and freedom of life-style, subject only to minimal constraints. This minimum he finds at the point where the individual's freedom threatens that of other people. Finding, as he does, a defence of these values to be compatible with utilitarianism, another source of Mill's individualism can be found in that utilitarianism itself. For while Mill qualified utilitarian theory in respect of recognising different qualities of happiness as potential social goals, and recognised, too, superiority of learning and of judgement, he did not qualify the basic utilitarian premiss of the equality of persons, or the equal value of all individuals.

Mill, therefore, in observing the risks to individual freedom paradoxically inherent in democracy itself, was concerned to propose boundaries of individual freedom over which it should be recognised that no one, and certainly not the organised state, had the right to trespass. The problem which he perceived was that of defining the nature and limits of the power which can legitimately be exercised by society over the individual. Democracy, he said, had shown that such phrases as 'self-government' and 'the power of the people over themselves' do not express the true state of affairs. Instead, 'the "people" who exercise the power are not always the same people as those over whom it is exercised; and the "self-government" spoken of is not the government of each by himself, but of each by all the rest'.[8]

The tyranny of the majority, then, is, Mill believed, a permanent hazard of democracy, and as such, something to be guarded against as much as any of the more typical historical forms of tyranny. This includes, in Mill's view, tyranny of opinion, as much as physical compulsion - the 'tendency of society to impose, by means other than civil penalties, its own ideas and rules of conduct on those who dissent from them'.[9] Mill insists that external acts affecting other people are the only legitimate object of coercion; the sphere of freedom is 'that portion of a person's life and conduct which affects only himself, or, if it affects others, only with their free, voluntary and undeceived consent and participation'.[10] The sphere of activity affecting only oneself, Mill defines as:

(1) the inward domain of consciousness,
(2) one's tastes and pursuits,
(3) association with other individuals.

The first of these is the most important, since the liberties demanded under this head are: liberty of conscience; liberty of thought and feeling; and absolute freedom of opinion on all subjects, practical or speculative, scientific, moral, or theological. In his classic argument for toleration of opinion, Mill examines the three possibilities that the opinion in question may be (a) true, (b) false, or (c) partly true and partly false. Those who insist that a view is not true and try to suppress it for this reason are, says Mill, claiming infallibility. If it is true, then they are depriving the human race of something of value. But in the event that the opinion expressed is false, the cause of truth is equally harmed because the truth to which the opinion is opposed will be held only as a dead dogma.

Later Mill carries his argument further, saying that people should be free to *act* on their opinions. He says: 'As it is useful that while mankind is imperfect there should be different opinions, so it is that there should be different experiments in living.'[11] Conformity is in itself a bad thing, Mill argues, commenting that to do things simply because it is the custom is to use only the faculty shared with the lower animals, that of imitation. It is only in the exercise of choice, Mill urges, that a human being uses his peculiar mental and moral powers. Otherwise, he says:

> the mind itself is bowed to the yoke: even in what people do for pleasure, conformity is the first thing thought of; they like in crowds; they exercise choice only among things commonly done: peculiarity of taste, eccentricity of conduct, are shunned equally with crimes: until by dint of not following their own nature they have no nature to follow: their human capacities are withered and starved.[12]

By contrast, Mill believed that individuality makes human life rich, diversified and animating. In favour of this view he argues that originality and genius are socially useful; that the amount of eccentricity in a society has generally been proportional to the amount of genius, mental vigour and moral courage it contained; that human beings differ and unless allowed to live differently will not be able to find happiness or develop to the full their personalities; and that nations cease to be progressive when they cease to permit individuality.

Mill admits that the state is entitled to exact some code of conduct from the individual in return for the benefits it confers on him, but he denies that state interference can ever be justified on grounds of looking after the interest or the moral welfare of the individual himself. The objection that it is in practice impossible to draw a line between the part of a person's conduct which affects others and that which affects only himself is resisted by Mill on the ground of a distinction between cause and effect. The *cause* of a man's failure to maintain his family - alcoholism, for example - is within the first realm and not the state's business. The *effect* - the failure to maintain - is a social duty and rightly open to regulation. Other causes might produce the same result; other effects might flow from the same cause. Finally, Mill produces three arguments against state interference, even when this interference is not an assault on liberty:

(1) What is done is likely to be done better by individuals than by the government.
(2) Doing the thing themselves is likely to strengthen and educate the individuals concerned.
(3) It is a direct evil to add anything unnecessarily to the power of the state.

Mill's views are summed up at the end of his essay on liberty in a passage which reflects his main arguments:

> The worth of a State, in the long run, is the worth of the individuals composing it; and a State which postpones the interests of *their* mental expansion and elevation to a little more of administrative skill, or of that semblance of it which practice gives, in the details of business; a State which dwarfs its men, in order that they may be more docile instruments in its hands even for beneficial purposes - will find that with small men no great thing can really be accomplished; and that the perfection of machinery to which it has sacrificed everything will in the end avail it nothing, for want of the vital power which, in order that the machine might work more smoothly, it has preferred to banish.[13]

It would not be appropriate here, and it is not the intention, to embark upon a critical examination of the views of Mill and Marx. Instead, the contrast described at the outset can now be drawn in more precise terms, and some indication given of the key points at which these two influential ideologies confront each other.

To begin with, we may take the differing approaches to ideology itself, or, more generally, to truth. For the Marxist, the vital questions to ask when a system of thought is at issue are not 'Does it accord with the facts?' or 'Is its logical basis sound?' but 'How did it arise?', 'Who benefits from its acceptance?'. A preoccupation with the psychological and social origins of a belief overwhelms and supersedes any investigation of the accuracy, correctness, agreement with facts or rationally argued basis of the belief. So, for example, in current educational debate, discussion of the validity of a given view concerning forms of knowledge may be over-ridden by examination of the social and cultural position of those holding that point of view.

The second question - who benefits? - suggests a form of pragmatism. But pragmatism, as the view that a true theory is one that works - one that bears fruitful results in practice - has an unacceptable objectivity by the standards of the position under discussion. For here benefit is located in the dominant class, and a position first adopted by Thrasymachus in Plato's dialogue, the *Republic,* is presumed. Thrasymachus had expressed his view in these terms: 'In all states alike "right" has the same meaning, namely what is for the interest of the party established in power, and that is the strongest.'[14] This position is narrower than the one being described here in that in the passage from the *Republic* it is the moral 'right' that is in question, while the contemporary argument extends more generally to answer Pontius Pilate's widest of all questions, 'What is truth?'. The answer implied is that truth is whatever the dominant group in society chooses to say is true.

Mill's view, on the other hand, takes as its premiss the objectivity of truth, in a sense which comes closer to the notion of truth as correspondence with the facts. Mill's commitment to the pursuit of truth as something lying outside the ability of man to create it, something which imposes its own constraints, and may even be unwelcome, dangerous, and socially and personally damaging in its implications, but is none the less worth pursuing in spite of this, is revealed in such passages as these:

> Who can compute what the world loses in the multitude of promising intellects with timid characters, who dare not follow out any bold, vigorous, independent train of thought, lest it should land them in something which would admit of being considered irreligious or immoral? . . . No-one can be a great thinker who does not recognise, that as a thinker it is his first duty to follow his intellect to whatever conclusions it may lead.[15]

> When an opinion is true, it may be extinguished once, twice, or many times, but in the course of ages there will generally be found persons to rediscover it, until some one of its reappearances falls on a time when from favourable circumstances it escapes persecution until it has made such head as to withstand all subsequent attempts to suppress it.[16]

This contrast is reinforced by looking at the narrower question of moral truth or ethical values. The Marxist position is characterised by the repudiation of abstract norms of morality and is strongly relativistic. Kamenka quotes Marx as saying 'conscience is related to the knowledge and whole way of life of a man. A republican has a different conscience from a Royalist, a propertied man has a different conscience from one who is propertyless, a thoughtful man a different one from a man without thought.'[17] In other words, as Kamenka comments, there is no morality, only moralities. And indeed this must follow from the position assigned to morality as part of the superstructure shaped solely by material and economic factors. For an important aspect of morality, in the abstract sense of which Kant is perhaps the best exponent, is its ability to operate as a cause or motivation for human conduct - a principle of conduct which defies any scientific or deterministic analysis of behaviour in terms of satisfaction of material desires.

The form of utilitarianism to which Mill was the heir and which had been worked out in detail by Bentham also found the springs of human action in the maximisation of pleasure and the avoidance of pain, so that it, too, offered a naturalistic account of ethics. Mill himself, however, as has been indicated earlier, defended a range of values which, while they might be ultimately justifiable in terms of utility, were for the present valid and binding in their own right.

It may well be the case that contemporary liberalism would gain much in consistency and conviction by presenting itself clearly as a system involving a plurality of values, and it is arguable that the failure to adopt such a view explains many of the well-known inconsistencies in Mill's own position. The contrast that emerges, then, is one between a materialistic and deterministic ethic on the one hand and a commitment to specified moral and social values on the other. As a consequence, defence of freedom of conscience will be an important aspect of the second system but an unjustifiable triviality for the first.

This leads to what is perhaps the most important aspect of the two ideologies under discussion. There is an essentially democratic element in the view that each man may be, as far as possible, his own judge of truth in general and ethical value in particular. Marx, by contrast, saw the individualism that was possible within the modern state as essentially egotistical, human rights needing to be claimed only within an unbalanced society, and carrying, moreover, an unacceptable implication that man was in control of his own destiny. As Graeme Duncan sums up this position: 'Men assert their individuality only against others and against society. Their apparent independence is actually indifference - "independence, that is, to collide with one another freely and to barter within the limits of this freedom".'[18]

Where the rights and independence of the individual are made light of, whatever the intention, it is the state which is likely to fill the vacuum created, so that the relative importance attached to self-determination within specified limits, or to state domination and control, follows from the value or lack of value accorded to the individual conscience.

The relativism which gives rise to the Marxist position, however, is convincing only when certain factors are ignored. A foremost consideration must be the timespan and continuity of Western culture, in which ethical and epistemological discussion have progressed without reference to the many different economic orders of society which have succeeded each other over the course of two millenniums.

Secondly, there are important logical difficulties in presenting a coherent relativism, difficulties encountered by Engels and Lenin as they turned their attention from bourgeois morality to the concept of morality in a communist society.[19] Relativism involves an attempt, logically doomed to failure, to step outside one's own frame of reference and pronounce in a dispassionate way that the theory itself condemns as impossible, upon the judgements of others.

Thirdly, it could be maintained that Kuhn's arguments on the structure of scientific revolutions and the recent development of non-Euclidean geometries and alternative systems of logic have altered approaches to science and mathematics respectively, in a way which could be seen as lending support to the Marxist analysis of knowledge. But there is still in practical terms a degree of objectivity and testability involved in these areas which undermines any facile and unsophisticated epistemological relativism.

The protection and safeguarding of individual judgement is, as has already been suggested, a principle which is directly connected with the view that what men think is important in practical terms. Mill wrote 'One person with a belief is a social power equal to ninety-nine who have only interests' and 'It is how men think that determines how they act'.[20] For this reason Mill's form of individualism was one which valued spontaneity and even eccentricity. The Marxist view, however, places the individual in the position of a puppet of forces outside his own control. As far as education is concerned, two very different ideals are implied. The ideal of education that Mill explicitly pressed was an ideal of education for critical judgement. The determinist view, however, suggests an ideal of education to secure 'right' thinking - a concept which has come to the fore under twentieth-century totalitarianism, most notably as the dominating feature of education in China under the cultural revolution.

The application to education of the contrast discussed in the present chapter must be developed more fully in the next. It has been suggested here, however, that it is a contrast best understood as set within the context and framework of alternative forms of society, so that the theoretical questions 'Which ideals do we value?', 'Which approach represents the truth?' become externalised in the question 'What sort of society do we want?'. Their application to education lies in the fact that the education system is the seed-pod of the society we seek to create or preserve, so that in the shaping of the education system lies the shaping of the future political and social order.

NOTES: CHAPTER 7

1   F. W. Garforth (ed.), *Mill's Educational Writings* (Columbia, NY: Teachers College Press, Columbia University, 1971), p. 186.
2   J. S. Mill, *On Liberty* (London: Dent, Everyman, 1954), pp. 72-3.
3   K. Marx, *The Poverty of Philosophy* (Moscow: Foreign Languages Publishing House, 1962), p. 197.
4   J. J. Rousseau, *Emile* (London: Dent, Everyman, 1966), p. 5.
5   See M. Young (ed.), *Knowledge and Control, New Directions for the Sociology of Education* (London: Collier Macmillan, 1971) for a collection of essays written from this standpoint.
6   Mill, op. cit., p. 74.
7   J. S. Mill, *Utilitarianism* (London: Dent, Everyman, 1954), p. 55.
8   Mill, *On Liberty,* p. 67.
9   ibid., p. 68.
10 ibid., p. 75.
11 ibid., p. 115.
12 ibid., p. 119.
13 ibid., p. 170.
14 F. M. Cornford, *The Republic of Plato* (London: Oxford University Press, 1955), p. 18.
15 Mill, *On Liberty,* p. 94.
16 ibid., p. 90.
17 E. Kamenka, *Marxism and Ethics* (London: Macmillan, 1969), p. 32.
18 G. Duncan, *Marx and Mill* (Cambridge: Cambridge University Press, 1973), p. 88. The quotation is from Marx's *Grundrisse.*
19 For a further consideration of the logical problems involved in ethical relativism see discussion in Chapter 9 and also B. Cohen, 'Three ethical fallacies', *Mind,* vol. 86 (1977).
20 J. S. Mill, *Representative Government* (London: Dent, Everyman, 1955), pp. 183-4.

Chapter 8

Education in a Liberal Society

The contrast between Mill and Marx has illustrated two very different social ideals, one oriented to the individual, the other to a conception of personal life subordinate to and dominated by overwhelming political and social controls. Few, as individuals, would opt for life under the second description, except in so far as they have become convinced of its inevitability, or, alternatively, have so closed their minds to the logic of their own position that they are inspired by the thought of their own capacity, as individuals, to bring about and assume leading positions in such a society. To the many paradoxes, then, generated by the notion of freedom may be added this: that only error or misunderstanding would lead a free individual to prefer a state-dominated to an individual-oriented society, since this one initial choice would pre-empt all further exercise of choice in areas of importance. If one is committed to the notion of choice, then, and persuaded of its possibility, the question of what are the conditions for the maintenance of the individual-oriented society will be of first importance.

It was suggested at the outset that those interested in the creation or perpetuation of such a society would need to identify those features of a liberal society which were relevant to education - those wider social principles which would need to be reflected in the organisation and structure of education if the gains of one generation were not to be blindly sacrificed by the next through ignorance of their true import and meaning. Put in the most basic terms, this is the question of what sort of education we need for the sort of society we want - if the capacity to choose a particular social order in preference to another is to be preserved.

The contrast in ideologies just presented makes it possible to see what some of these features must be. Before identifying these, however, some support needs to be given to the notion of a reciprocal relation between education and society, in which education appears as reflecting society, and society as mirroring education. For it would be easy to fall into the error of conceiving of the educational experience of the young as a closed system, whether or not such a conception is formed from a viewpoint of optimism or pessimism. The favourable or optimistic view of education as a closed system is that such isolation is beneficial in its effects, with different and purer values being instilled into the young in spite of the corruption and worldliness of the wider life of the community. Pessimistically viewed, on the other hand, the isolation could be taken as supplying a situation in which unreasonable and unproductive values flourish in the despotic closed community of schools, where adult life awaits with a promise of personal self-fulfilment and well-being. But neither the optimistic nor the pessimistic view can be justified, for schools are the product of particular forms of society and reflect their preoccupations and presumptions.

Two examples illustrate this well. English boarding-school life as portrayed in nineteenth-century novels by authors such as Talbot Baines Reed was largely supplied and serviced by people with no experience of the wider world opening up to the Victorian English. And yet what better or more appropriate preparation could have been devised for the overseas military, explorational, or missionary adventures of the era? For the frequently lonely and invariably arduous exploits in these fields for which the period is famous, a first requirement was for self-sufficient individuals who were emotionally and physically independent of family and friendship ties, accustomed to living with attachment to no more possessions than could be carried on the person, with expectations not geared to physical comfort or softness, and a range of values which included team-spirit, fortitude, courage, emotional control, as well as the qualities of leadership and strategic planning. In a very direct sense it could be said that the hardness and trials of life in Victorian educational establishments - although these would undoubtedly be the subject of considerable sympathy if transposed into the late twentieth century - prepared those who experienced them for the rigours and hardships characteristic of the era.

Similarly, in the mid-twentieth century and earlier (in the period between the two world wars and during and after the Second World War) a contrast can be drawn between schools in America which were psychologically as well as physically removed from the European militaristic climate, and schools in some of the countries in Europe in which the dominant feature was an emphasis on practices appropriate to societies at war. In England uniforms and badges, although defended on all kinds of other grounds, including benevolent concern for the poor and for the obliteration of class distinction within the school, were none the less signs of a military orientation, and whether intentionally or not provided the appropriate preparation for those who would leave school and take their place in a branch of the military services. The emphasis on uniform was reinforced with drilling, lining-up, strict discipline, silent obedience and doing everything in well-ordered groupings to bells and signals.

These two examples do, of course, support to some extent the 'hidden curriculum' argument mentioned earlier, but without its sinister or 'conspiracy theory' overtones. There is a direct link between the values and preoccupations of school and the values and preoccupations of society, a point which has received some empirical substantiation in the development of humanistic sociology. This is an approach to sociological inquiry which has been pursued by some Polish sociologists and, although set within a framework of Marxism, takes as its starting-point the need to accept the reality of human values and attitudes as facts.[1]

This link was recognised, too, by John Dewey, writing in the very different time and context of late nineteenth- and early twentieth-century America. It was the political and social, rather than purely moral values of democracy which he related to the educational process. In particular he drew a contrast between an aristocratic order of society, on the one hand, and a democratic order on the other. He saw the first as involving a minority of people living on inherited wealth and not engaging in manual labour and thus generating a culturally ornamental but practically useless non-vocational form of education for these few; the second as based on co-operative work, both manual and non-manual, and thus requiring a more practically oriented, vocationally relevant form of education, specifically involving groupwork, practical activities and a problem-centred approach.[2]

Dewey, however, was himself living too close to the dividing line which he so acutely drew between the old and the new to see that the new - the democratic order - was itself divided. It was left to Talmon, in the aftermath of the Second World War, to identify an ambiguity in the notion of democracy summed up in the distinction he drew between the alternative concepts of liberal and totalitarian democracy - a distinction which he described as the most vital of our time. It is this distinction which underlies the contrast which has been discussed above, for it is this contrast within a democratic framework, rather than between a democratic system and some other, that features in the problem areas for education that have been discussed in earlier chapters. The difference in attitudes to politics which is involved is described by Talmon in these words:

The liberal approach assumes politics to be a matter of trial and error, and regards political systems as pragmatic contrivances of human ingenuity and spontaneity. It also recognises a variety of levels of personal and collective endeavour, which are altogether outside the sphere of politics.

The totalitarian democratic school, on the other hand, is based upon the assumption of a sole and exclusive truth in politics . . . It widens the scope of politics to embrace the whole of human existence. It treats all human thought and action as having social significance, and therefore falling within the orbit of political action . . .

Both schools affirm the supreme value of liberty. But whereas one finds the essence of freedom in spontaneity and the absence of coercion, the other believes it to be realized only in the pursuit and attainment of an absolute collective purpose.[3]

Talmon goes on to pose the question: 'Is human freedom compatible with an exclusive pattern of social existence, even if this pattern aims at the maximum of social justice and security?' This crucial question suggests another which might be raised within the narrower context of education: 'Are political and social freedom compatible with an exclusive pattern of educational provision, even if this pattern aims at a maximum of social justice?' This is to return to the question, raised at the outset, of what characteristics are imposed on the structure and form of an educational system by a desire to promote a liberal society. Talmon's question suggests that as far as the *structure* of the educational system is concerned, the first such characteristic must be the avoidance of coercion, even in the interests of achieving a desirable and socially advantageous outcome. Hence the first priority within a liberal society must be the preservation of areas of retreat for those who, for one reason or another, cannot be persuaded to share the consensus view of what education should be.

The individual families discussed earlier, even if they are to be criticised as wrong-headed or misguided, or as not acting in the narrowly conceived best interests of their children, are claiming and maintaining a right which it is impossible for a liberal society to sacrifice and still maintain its distinctively individualist character. Independent schools and religious foundations, even if, on the most unfavourable assumptions, their impact is socially distorting and even if they offer an education which a secular, democratically minded rationalist would find less than ideal, are reinforcing the emphasis on individual choice and the absence of coercion which are essential hallmarks of a non-totalitarian society. By their sheer variety they provide a check, a dispersal of power, preventing concentration of control in a centralised source. They also represent, together with the parental freedom to stand outside the system altogether, a crucial bastion against the possibility of an education system being used for purposes of moral and political indoctrination.

These implications for the organisation of education are derived from reflection on the notion of personal liberty as the prime characteristic of liberalism, and it is important to consider whether any other structural consequences follow from the same characteristic. Personal freedom is for political purposes commonly spelt out in more concrete terms and held to include freedom of thought, freedom of speech and publication, freedom of association and freedom of worship - freedoms which are important in relation to the form and content of education as well as to its organisational structure. To these may be added freedom to pursue an occupation. The significance of this freedom for education lies in the fact that it can be linked to the need to provide equal educational opportunities, or perhaps even equal education. Hobhouse drew the former conclusion in his classic essay on liberalism, when he wrote: 'Freedom to choose and follow an occupation, if it is to be fully effective, means equality with others in the opportunities for following such occupation.'[4] This freedom, which essentially involves the principle of an 'open road for talent', is indeed a liberal ideal, but one, nevertheless, which need not be interpreted so as to operate against its more central tenets, since its demands can, in fact, be met within the framework suggested here, without involving monolithic centralised educational organisation.

These conditions of freedom, then, help to sketch in the outlying shape within which the more detailed picture of education in a liberal society is to be set. But before considering this more detailed picture, it is necessary to take account of a more extreme position. This is the position of those who would pursue the above argument beyond acceptance of the external and organisational conditions which have been suggested here to a point which denies altogether the need for state participation and intervention. If this extreme conclusion is to be avoided, then the claims that have so far been made for resisting a state monopoly in education will need to be balanced by some consideration of the grounds that exist for regarding the state as having a legitimate interest in education, and for stopping short of a demand that the state should remain outside the educational process altogether.

At a minimum, there is very general agreement that education should be compulsory. In this basic respect children are viewed in abstraction from their parents, and the moral obligation of society as a whole to ensure the education of all children without exception is expressed as a right of all children to education. The relationship between obligations on the one hand and rights on the other will be discussed later. At this point it is important to recognise that compulsory education historically and practically means free education. Children cannot usually provide for their own education and it would be meaningless to impose on their parents an obligation which their personal circumstances might make it impossible for them to fulfil. So at least as long as the principle of compulsory education is recognised, state funding of education at least for those unable to make their own provision follows as a necessary consequence.

Milton Friedman in discussing this issue puts forward two arguments which would justify state intervention in education, even for a liberal who favours the minimal state in its most extreme form.[5] The first of these is a socio-economic argument concerning what are technically called 'neighbourhood effects'. These are circumstances where the action of one individual imposes costs on others for which it is not feasible to make him compensate them; or else which yield gains to others for which it is not feasible to make *them* compensate *him*. His second argument is an argument from paternalism - a concern for the young or irresponsible.

The second of these arguments is self-explanatory and widely accepted. The first requires some explanation. 'Neighbourhood effects' in education consist in the fact that educating children contributes to the general welfare by creating a stable democratic society, since a minimum degree of literacy, knowledge and shared values is necessary for this, while education beyond this minimum, at least for some, is justified by the need for good social and political leadership. The case Friedman is making is limited, since he does not believe that these grounds justify subsidising vocational training, nor in general higher education, the cost of which Friedman believes should fall on the recipient, through student loans or other means.

The practical conclusion he draws for the other areas of education where he considers state provision to be justified is that, while the principle of subsidy is established, there is no reason why the state should also provide and administer schooling. He therefore recommends the more direct form of financial provision represented by a voucher system in which parents would be enabled to choose between institutions, so long as these met the minimum standards established by the state.

Given these recommendations, it is interesting to compare the views of Friedman, who is widely regarded as a politically conservative economic and social theorist, with those of Illich whose academic and political position stands in sharp contrast. Illich has been particularly identified with a concern for underprivileged ethnic minorities in industrialised urban societies and with the interests of Third World rural communities, and is perhaps best known for his rejection of the organised educational system in *De-Schooling Society*. He argued there that school is the paradigm instance of the institutionalisation of values, a process which in developed societies occurs equally in the areas of health, mobility and religion. In all these areas and more particularly in the area of education he suggests that non-material needs are turned into demands for commodities. But because he considers that education polarises society creating a wealthy educated class and generating consumer expectations, he comes to conclusions which overlap to a surprising extent with those of Friedman.

Both are against a state-supervised system of licensing teachers (the creation of a class of certificated professionals), although Illich goes further than Friedman in objecting to teaching itself as a necessary aspect of the process of learning. He goes further, too, in a much wider objection to educational qualifications as requirements for any form of employment. Both query the necessity for the state to provide whatever education is agreed to be required, as opposed to merely providing a financial subsidy. Both, in fact, offer the same solution to this problem in proposing the provision of educational vouchers to be cashed according to choice and inclination.

Another advocate of the minimal state, Nozick, whose general position was discussed earlier, would draw its boundaries even more narrowly than would Friedman, so that paternalistic educational provision would fall outside these boundaries. To draw the line at the point where Nozick would draw it, however, between what the state should provide and what should be left to the individual is not a practical option within the highly complex forms of society in which most people with an interest in such theoretical questions either live or aspire to live. It fails not only to take account of Friedman's 'neighbourhood effect' principle, but also of the justifiability of paternalism when applied to its natural recipients, the young, who cannot be regarded as the property of their parents, but as potential full members of society whose potentiality needs to be safeguarded and developed.

In forming a conception, then, of the conditions which ought to govern education in a liberal society, the argument that education may be left to chance and the whim of individuals may be discounted. The free availability of education is an essential aspect of a liberal society and a prior condition for the sophisticated and highly participatory form of political life that democratic liberalism involves. The structure and form of that provision, however, need to be such as to protect and enhance individual liberty. So far it has been argued that this is best achieved if education is allowed under many different forms both within and outside a formal state-provided system.

It is possible to add to this conclusion that within a structure which leaves a maximum of initiative to the individual the question of size of establishments is an important ancillary matter, for clearly the maximisation of choice is related to the number and variety of alternatives available. It follows that schools should be as small as is consistent with efficiency and success in functioning. It follows, too, that in order to encourage the development of such a range of alternatives, direct rather than indirect payment is to be preferred - in other words, the voucher system, or some variant of it, is dictated as an important connecting link in the fabric of liberal educational provision, even if its practicability has in the end to be accepted as determined on grounds of expediency and economic practicability rather than principle.

These considerations of structural framework have, however, all been related to a single characteristic of liberalism - the value it places on liberty. Other aspects of liberalism, while having some relevance to organisational structure, are also important in relation to the form and content of education in a free society. One such aspect is the respect for the individual which distinguishes liberalism from other political systems. This feature of liberalism dictates a character of universality of application for the workings of the education systems which parallels the universality it demands in the area of legal rights. Marking out groups or individuals by reference to ethnic origin, colour, or social class is essentially a partisan practice which is foreign to the principle of impartiality expressed in the Kantian phrase 'respect for persons'. Positive discrimination, then, based on such principles of demarcation will be ruled out except in so far as such provision can be expressed in general terms. For example, the principle of impartiality is being violated if a university decides to admit students on special terms because they belong to a particular racial group; it is not being violated if those same students are admitted on specially favourable terms because they left school early without educational qualifications. For the second condition may be met by anybody; the first involves the kind of discrimination which has been recognised as a violation of the principle of respect for the individual in the negative forms which it has taken in the past. To substitute a positive form is no less invidious.

A third important characteristic of liberalism is that it is a system involving a plurality of moral principles. This is frequently expressed in terms of a search for human rights, for a rational human morality, or for universal values. This aspect will be discussed in the next chapter, but at this point it is the question of the implications of the liberal perspective for the form and content of education which is at issue, and on which some conclusions may now be proposed.

On what principles, then, should the inner shape of education be determined in a liberal society? As a point of departure, Hobhouse's dictum that it is 'the function of the State to secure the conditions upon which mind and character may develop themselves' may be accepted as prior presumption.[6] But the way in which this is to be achieved must be more precisely defined. The question was considered by Mill, who had a direct personal interest in education. He believed that human nature was pliable, and believed too in the 'unlimited possibility of improving the moral and intellectual condition of mankind by education'.[7] This belief in the possibility of improvement would seem to be essential, though it need not entail a belief in perfectibility, nor a preference for a Lamarckian, rather than Darwinian, biological viewpoint. Mill himself linked closely the notions of knowledge, virtue and social cohesion, although his hopes for education and a cohesive social morality backed and sanctioned by enlightened public opinion must be set against his defence of the individual in the face of the 'hostile and dreaded censorship' of intrusive social control.

Accepting the spirit of these observations, however, it would seem that there is a clear implication of liberal thought that the first condition for education in a free society - one based on tolerance and individual self-determination - is that it should be critical rather than conformist, and that it should aim at individual autonomy rather than social control. A conception of education as involving the development of capacities of rational thought and critical appraisal could be argued to be intrinsic to the notion of education rather than an extrinsic requirement of a particular type of society. But this underlines the essential inseparability of social and educational ideals already discussed. The values of society are and must be the values of its education system; the values of an education system are and must be the values of society.

The commitment to freedom and toleration which entails an education critical and inquiring in its form might seem to involve educational freedom in a narrower sense - the sense associated with progressive education. From this point of view, it might be linked with particular classroom strategies - informal teaching methods, group-work and working from independent materials, self-timetabling, or even unsupervised self-chosen activities. But to derive practical techniques from principle as closely as this would be a mistake.

There is a conception of progressive education which particularly values the autonomy of the individual, and those who favour it can reasonably argue that it is a form well-suited to a liberal society. (And it is indeed the case that educational strategies of this sort are and have been positively outlawed in totalitarian societies). But C. D. Hardie's comment on Dewey's progressivism is worth recalling here: that it may be the case that an autocratic educational system is necessary to secure a democratic society.[8] This is because a free society is a sophisticated rather than a simple organism and depends on procedures and approaches which need to be positively and consciously developed rather than coming naturally to human beings. Otherwise examples of free societies would not be confined to a few isolated cases, largely of recent emergence and in geographically confined areas, but would have been the norm for social organisation across many epochs and civilisations. Since this is patently not so, the defender of a liberal society will not be inconsistent if, while avoiding indoctrination and education for conformity, and while encouraging inquiry, criticism and impartial appraisal of different opinions, he applies himself to the task of education in a firm and positive way. To quote Hobhouse again: 'nor is liberty opposed to discipline, to organisation, to strenuous conviction as to what is true and just'.[9]

The individualist values of self-determination and autonomy, then, will not need to be enshrined in a progressive rather than a traditional approach to education, although they may be; and the traditional approach itself will need to be based on these values rather than on the total swamping of the individual's personality which has been a feature of some traditional schooling, especially in a boarding context. In particular any form of education adopted in a liberal society must respect the essential freedoms of spirit involved in the areas of morals, religion and politics.

Secondly, respect for the developing individual entails within the liberal, and therefore plural, society, the cultivation of a variety of talent. The valuing of such a variety of talent, which was inseparable in Mill's thought from the defence of liberty and toleration, is a feature of a society which has turned its back on the enforced cultivation of homogeneity and uniformity. While the distribution of individual talent is arbitrary, it is by no means morally indifferent, and no moral principle requires its suppression or a policy of levelling out of abilities. The moral requirement, on the contrary, is for the identification of special talent and for its development to its fullest potential.

This points to a third consequence for education implicit in the notion of a liberal society. For if diversity of talent is to be fostered, then the syllabus offered within schools must be wide enough to permit this. Thus a liberal education in the traditional sense is a prerequisite of a liberal society. In other words, it is important that no main area of human thought or enterprise is omitted from the curriculum. This does not imply a common curriculum throughout the years of schooling, but it does rule out both early specialisation and also some forms of progressive organisation which are insufficiently structured to guarantee each student's full educational experiences.

Fourthly, the conditions attaching to the education of women must be spelt out separately. For in this area particularly it cannot be taken for granted that what is conceded as applying in general will be taken to apply in the same way to both women and men, boys and girls. Just as universal suffrage can be taken to mean votes for all men but no women, so these universal requirements for education will in some societies be interpreted as valid for males but not for females. Even where the principle of substantially the same education is conceded, an insistence that this should be supplied separately in separate institutions - even, as in some Muslim countries, by female teachers only - means that the effective integration of women in the intellectual life of the community is in practice prevented. If women are to play a part in a society's culture, then educational institutions at higher levels must be integrated and open equally to both sexes; neither can the basic requirements of liberalism be met without free exchange and contact between people irrespective of sex.

Fifthly, and finally, the principle of academic freedom is directly linked with the notion of a liberal society, since to value criticism and open inquiry is to value what must be their prerequisite, the freedom to speak and to teach on subjects and in ways which are not subject to external interference and control. This must rule out centralised control of the curriculum, although an agreed policy and approach on curriculum matters is both defensible and rational. The pursuit of such a policy, however, should not be pushed to the point of compulsion even if this means that in some situations educational absurdities will occur. The best protection against these educational absurdities is the freedom as a last resort to dissociate oneself and one's children from the education offered by the state.

These, then, are the educational consequences of a commitment to the values of liberalism. They give some kind of indication of the features which need to be safeguarded or fostered in the face of overzealous attempts at imposing an ideal education system conceived in other terms and in pursuit of other values. These other values may include equality, the promotion of happiness, even fraternity. All may be worth pursuing, but it is important to be clear that, whatever their virtues, these are not the primary values within which the concept of liberalism is set. The primary values of liberalism are freedom and toleration; self-determination and autonomy; individual judgement, criticism and originality. And a society which values these needs to maintain a keen vigilance if other and subsidiary values are not to gain a dominating and controlling ascendancy first at the level of education and then in the wider society, transforming that society into another and alien entity.

NOTES: CHAPTER 8

1   For an application of this tradition to education see J. J. Smolicz, 'The concept of tradition: a humanistic interpretation', *The Australian and New Zealand Journal of Sociology,* vol. 10, no. 2 (1974), pp. 75-83.
2   J. Dewey, *Democracy and Education* (New York: Macmillan/The Free Press, 1916).
3   J. L. Talmon, *The Origins of Totalitarian Democracy* (London: Mercury Books, 1961), pp. 1-2.
4   L. T. Hobhouse, *Liberalism* (London: Oxford University Press, 1971), p. 21.
5   M. Friedman, *Capitalism and Freedom* (Chicago: University of Chicago Press, 1962), ch. 6.
6   Hobhouse, op. cit., p. 83.
7   J. S. Mill, *Autobiography* (London: Dent, Everyman, 1954), p. 91.
8   C. D. Hardie, 'The educational theory of John Dewey', in R. D. Archambault (ed.), *John Dewey on Education, Appraisals* (New York: Random House, 1966), p. 124.
9   Hobhouse, op. cit., p. 21.

Chapter 9

Human Rights: the International Understanding

Education within a liberal society has been considered here as an issue for people already living within such a society, and already committed to the perpetuation of its ideals and principles. But education as a practical activity is something which unites all human societies, and the liberal ideal, while it may be regarded in a particular context as a matter of personal or at least societal choice, includes elements which have wider, indeed universal, appeal. It is under this aspect that the value system of liberalism is frequently expressed in terms of human rights - moral rights attaching to persons in all orders of society, whether recognised by those societies or not.

While this is a notion of considerable contemporary significance, having been taken up and formalised by the international community, it is also a notion much older than liberalism itself or any form of liberal society. Its roots lie in the notion of natural law, which the Stoics opposed to the particular local law of communities, finding instead a moral imperative which imposed itself on man simply by virtue of his status as a human being and not as a member of a particular society. Such a moral imperative is conceived of as outweighing the laws of despots or even legitimate and benevolent rulers. While natural law must conform to man's deepest needs and aspirations, the arbitrary rules of human law-makers may be unjust or morally odious. Hence, although the Greeks themselves did not make the transition, the idea of natural law readily generates the notion of natural rights as marking out an area in which man-made laws, the laws of states, are subject to limits imposed by a wider conception of right. There is, then, implicit in these origins a conception of the privacy of the individual and respect for individual conscience. It was because it created this concept of an inner person independent of his social context that Stoicism was able to flourish as a slave philosophy, appealing to those most lacking in public or social recognition of their rights. The Roman notion of a *jus gentium* set this conception in a wider legal and political context, and it was reinforced by the respect for the individual which was the hallmark of the Christian religion.

The modern origins of the notion are traced by Kamenka to the execution of Charles I in 1649, an event which expressed the idea of judgement upon a king by the people in the name of a higher authority than even monarchical power.[1] More commonly it is found in the writings of the British philosopher John Locke, whose references to rights of life, liberty and property became the model on which were based both the American Declaration of Independence, which asserts inalienable rights to life, liberty and the pursuit of happiness, and the French Declaration of the Rights of Man and the Citizen issued in 1789, which recognises rights to liberty, property, security and resistance to oppression.

Contemporary declarations of rights have been considerably more detailed and far-reaching, taking the form of international agreements, some given legal force by the states endorsing them, others no more than statements of aspiration. The European Convention for the Protection of Human Rights and Fundamental Freedoms is an example of the first sort, with the International Court at The Hague available to judge cases which are presented to it. The United Nations' Universal Declaration of Human Rights is an example of the second sort, although supported by a more specific International Covenant on Economic, Social and Cultural Rights. Several writers have argued that these later declarations, marking as they do a shift in the direction of positive and welfare demands in contrast to the negative and protective emphasis of earlier statements, in fact debilitate and muddy the notion of rights. Before considering this charge, however, it is necessary in general terms to evaluate the notion of rights and to assess the claims of those who deny any meaningfulness at all to the notion.

The basis on which contemporary assertions of rights rest includes such fundamental moral attitudes as respect for human life; a belief in the dignity of the individual human being; a concern for the preservation of threatened species and for the long-term future of the planet as the heritage of future generations. These are claims which cannot be made wholly in terms of the restricted moral vocabulary of narrow obligation, but for which an all-embracing notion of the good is too vague and unspecific in its demands to give expression to the pressing nature of the considerations involved. The language of rights, then, stands in-between, covering both the exigency of the claims against us and their wide generality. For example, only the assertion of a right on the part of our descendants to an unpolluted planet expresses the obligation members of the present generation have in relation to the strategies they adopt now in environmental matters.

A moral vocabulary, then, which includes the notion of rights has a value as part of the fabric of human activity and goals. It is difficult to see, therefore, why anyone should wish to forfeit this notion. Part of the motivation for doing so, though, may be the presumption that such a notion can have no place in a hard-headed materialistic and scientific age which has largely rejected naive religious beliefs and primitive ethical taboos. This, however, is part of a general position which eschews moral concepts altogether, and before examining it, it would be worth considering the rather narrower view that while *some* moral concepts are valid, the concept of rights is redundant.

The idea that 'rights' might be redundant follows from reflecting on the traditional notion of a right as a correlative term to a duty. Moral philosophers at one time followed a standard division of duties into perfect and imperfect duties, the latter being duties such as charity which could be practised in an unspecified manner at the choice of the person concerned, the former being duties like promising which closed all other options and thus were seen as conferring a reciprocal right on another person. If this is the only pattern of rights, then it would indeed be the case that any reference to rights could be rephrased as a reference to duty or obligation.

Bradley urges strongly the view that rights and duties are completely correlative:

> No right without duty; no duty without right and rights . . . Right and duty are sides of a single whole. This whole is the good . . . Each is a single side of one and the same relation, fixed apart from the other side. In the good the sides come together, and in the whole first cease to be abstractions and gain real existence.[2]

While Bradley's suggestion that rights and duties are embedded in a wider notion of the good is one which it will be fruitful to develop, the idea that the two notions cannot function independently must be rejected. Two arguments may be advanced in justification of this rejection. First of all, even in relation to purely legal rights, which are both narrower and, as positive and determinable aspects of an existing legal system, of more readily acknowledged objectivity than moral rights, legal theorists have argued that the concept of a legal right is not redundant but allows individuals to make claims not covered by the notion of duty.[3] It is also the case that many of the things and forms of treatment to which individuals are acknowledged to be entitled in a constitutionally based society are not things or forms of treatment which they are entitled to receive from some particular person, and hence do not involve a particular individual in a specific duty. For example, my right to privacy is difficult to construe in terms of the duties of thousands of people who do not even know of my existence.

But secondly, and more important, where moral rights are concerned, it has been argued that the choice of the language of duty in preference to the language of rights is demeaning to the claimant. For example, to speak of the duties of slave-owners towards their slaves is a denial of the status of the slaves as people possessing rights against their owners. On this issue, Melden cites the impassioned remarks of the black abolitionist leader, Frederick Douglass, who asserted that

> the man who has *suffered the wrong* is the man to *demand redress* .
> . . the man *struck* is the man to *cry out* - and . . . he who has
> *endured the cruel pangs of slavery* is the man to *advocate Liberty*.
> It is evident that we must be our own representatives and
> advocates, not exclusively but peculiarly - not distinct from, but in
> connection with our white friends.[4]

In other words, people whose rights are denied to them are not seeking - what in a sense does not concern them - that others should conform to some moral ideal by carrying out their duties, but rather that their own entitlement should be secured to them, less by positive than by negative actions.

That the language of rights could effectively be abandoned, then, in favour of reference only to duty has yet to be demonstrated by those who hold that 'rights' talk is redundant. A more serious challenge, however, comes from those who reject moral notions altogether and sweep aside rights in a general rejection of ethical claims on conduct. Amongst these may be separately identified moral relativists, utilitarians (who, while offering an influential moral theory, nevertheless deny 'absolute' morality) and Marxists.

The relativist attack on the notion of rights stems from observation of the different attitudes and viewpoints accepted in different societies and the drawing of a hasty conclusion from this that no one of these viewpoints has more validity than any other. The conclusion is hastily drawn, however, when it is remembered that this was precisely the starting-point of the Greek concept of a natural law superseding the practices of different nations and states. It stems essentially from a logical confusion of types of statement. One may compare

No one should be subjected to torture

and

The claim that no one should be subjected to torture has no objective validity.

The distinction in question here is the distinction between the moral and meta-ethical. The first sentence is a moral assertion, uttered by someone actually engaging in the process of moral evaluation - a practising moral agent. The second is a meta-ethical assertion about the status of that moral utterance. The relativist attempts to deduce agnostic conclusions at the first level from his own agnosticism at the second level.

But the logic of moral discourse is such that anyone uttering a statement of the first sort is in fact by that very utterance aligning himself positively with the viewpoint expressed. If he goes on immediately to question its validity then he is withdrawing from that position or else, in continuing to maintain it, involving himself in the absurdity of contradictory assertions. It is only in the capacity of moral philosopher, moral commentator, or ethical anthopologist that he can make the second type of assertion, which will then leave entirely open the question of his own moral beliefs as a member of the moral community, a category which includes the whole human race.

The relativist will say, however, that it is precisely this wider universal membership that he sees as empty of moral significance, and he may choose to put this point in the form of a denial of absolute rights. Absolute rights may be contrasted with *prima facie* or presumed rights - rights which hold unless there are good reasons why they should be over-ridden (as, for instance, when there is a conflict of rights - property versus life, for example). But to recognise the possibility of conflict and therefore the necessity of compromise is not to confer the lower status on the notion of rights which is intrinsic to the relativist's position. Rights, in the sense under discussion here, must be absolute in that they are linked with the essential rather than merely local or socially-conditioned nature of man. The relativist, then, must be taken to be denying the existence of rights altogether as part of his insistence on the relativity of morality, and since this insistence can be shown to be logically incoherent, it follows that the relativist's rejection of rights is similarly flawed.

The position of the utilitarian leads to a rejection of rights on quite different grounds. Dating from Bentham's attack on rights as 'nonsense upon stilts', utilitarianism has been presented as a moral theory based on naturalism - based, that is, on conclusions which translate into publicly observable, empirically determined assertions about the consequence of actions or classes of actions for human happiness or satisfaction. Rights and other moral language seem to stand outside this scientific and practical framework and to make appeal to the metaphysical or the theological. This criticism, however, presupposes what it sets out to prove. If, indeed, everything of interest to men could be reduced to empirical terms, then utilitarianism would be one of the few moral theories which could be retained and translated into the favoured scientific language. But the impossibility of such a translation has been effectively demonstrated by G. E. Moore in his attack on naturalism and the naturalistic fallacy.[5] While the details of Moore's argument may be disputed, the historical importance of his attack on naturalism is that it is an assertion of the *sui generis* nature of moral concepts - their untranslatability into statements about the empirical facts of concrete situations or human psychological experiences.

For some, this will seem to detract from their status - unjustifiably, however, for if morality is accepted as providing another dimension of human experience and feeling, this is to recognise no more for it than might readily be conceded for the aesthetic domain, the religious domain, or the deeper world of human relationships as conveyed in great literary and dramatic works. So a straightforward denunciation of rights on the basis of utilitarian assumptions may be resisted by an equally straightforward assertion in the tradition of moral intuitionism that rights feature as an essential if abstract and indefinable part of the fabric of human existence, not to be translated away without residue into purely descriptive language.

The Marxist repudiation of rights has much in common with the utilitarian. The basic Marxist position of materialistic determinism is incompatible with the recognition of the metaphysical or moral status of rights, and in so far as the Marxist rejects rights on these grounds, the arguments against utilitarian materialism apply equally to it. Marxists, however, have made use of the notion of rights in various popular and revolutionary movements, and a new Marxist approach to the notion has evolved in which the notion of rights has been reinstated and reinterpreted. This has important implications which will be considered later. First, however, another criticism of rights from a basically sympathetic standpoint needs to be considered.

This position has been persuasively presented by John Kleinig who while recognising the advantages implicit in the notion of rights - advantages which include its long tradition, carrying with it respect and adding to its force and impact - suggests that it can today do more harm than good. He uses a biological analogy: some plant or animal species are occasionally introduced to a terrain in order to keep down pests, but eventually do this so effectively as to become greater pests themselves. This, he suggests, has become true to the notion of rights. He is critical, therefore, of the modern tendency, particularly in liberationist literature, to couch moral discussion in terms of rights (of blacks, of women, of children, for example). His own suggestion is that morality goes beyond rights, since these leave out such morally important things as love, care and compassion. 'There is', he says, 'something morally inadequate in doing something for another because it is the other's due. Actions motivated simply by the rights of others remain anonymous or impersonal, whereas if motivated by love, care or concern for the other their focus is on the other's particularity. Only relations of the latter kind are morally adequate. They are person-specific, whereas rights are "species"-specific.'[6]

This type of criticism has a great deal of point if one compares it with the position taken by Kant on rights. Kant wrote in denigration of the factors listed by Kleinig: 'if none of us ever did any act of love or charity but only kept inviolate the rights of everyman, there would be no misery in the world except sickness and misfortune, and other sufferings as do not spring from the violation of rights'.[7] One might add that there would be very little pleasure or happiness in the world either. However, while the point does have this emotional appeal, the fact is that rights belong much more to the area which has been the concern of this book, the area of relations between individual and state, than to the world of interpersonal relationships, where appeal to rights only appears when the warmer relationships which make such appeals unnecessary have broken down. The concept of political and social rights, then, should not be abandoned in the search for a more feeling-based personal morality.

If any moral notions are to be accepted, then, there is no reason why the notion of rights should be excluded. But without adopting any of the specific viewpoints that have so far been considered, someone who is not fully convinced of the case for rights may wish to raise the fundamental question, why should any moral notions be accepted? This is a question that can only be answered by accepting that the recognition of moral imperatives or moral ideals is essentially the recognition of a potential for man beyond the purely material. It is therefore to accept a particular view of the nature of man as a being capable of existence on two planes: the material level which is a necessary aspect of the fact that man is another animal species on the planet Earth; but also a higher and universal level, the essence of which is expressed in the notion of man as a moral being.

Such ideas, as put forward, for example, by Plato and Kant, have evolved within the same tradition of thought as that in which the concept of human rights has developed. The question of what it is that distinguishes man from the rest of nature has been answered in general in ways which are especially pertinent to education, particularly when education is recognised as having a moral as well as an intellectual aspect. Aristotle's concept of man as a 'rational animal' expresses an undeniable truth, and one foreshadowed perhaps in the Genesis allegory in which it is by eating fruit from the tree of knowledge that man and woman shed their innocence and that ability to live in a carefree thoughtless present which characterises other animals. Plamenatz presents a contemporary summary of such a view of what is distinctive in the nature of man:

> Man alone understands his condition and knows his limitations; he alone has purposes as well as desires; he alone among God's creatures here on earth can conceive of a life worth living, can want to be one kind of person rather than another. He alone is ambitious, provident, conscientious, and aspiring. He alone can know what freedom is and can want it and respect it in others.[8]

A conception of morality, then, lies embedded in such a conception of the nature of humanity. Morality, however, in this fundamental sense is optimally expressed in particular social and political settings. And the liberal moral ideal, while it might be expressible otherwise, finds one form of expression in the doctrine of natural or human rights and this can only be fully realised in a political context where these rights are respected and recognised.

Since this ideal includes a level of awareness, intelligence and information, together with the development of attitudes favourable to its own preservation, those rights which are especially relevant to education have particular importance. It would be easy to assume that it is positive rights *to* education which are of key importance here, but it will be clear to anyone who has pursued the argument so far that any such positive right must be qualified by the negative rights, founded on a much longer tradition of political and moral thought, which are also relevant to the concept of education. Reference was made earlier to the charge that modern declarations of rights are confused and confusing in that they merge calls for negative rights to liberty and non-interference with positive calls for economic and social welfare - confused demands because the first set limits to state interference, while the second make necessary the vast bureaucracy and centralised control of the modern state, with invasions of privacy and heavy taxation of income as necessary concomitants.

It is worth, therefore, setting out those parts of the Universal Declaration of Human Rights, and other international agreements, which are especially relevant to the issue of education. On the negative side the Universal Declaration of Human Rights states:

> No one shall be subjected to arbitrary interference with his privacy, family, home or correspondence . . . (Article 12)

The family is the natural and fundamental group unit of society and is entitled to protection by society and the State. (Article 16, 3)

On the positive side, the Declaration includes the following:

Everyone . . . is entitled to realisation . . . of the economic, social and cultural rights indispensable for his dignity and the free development of his personality. (Article 22)

Everyone has the right to education. (Article 26, 1)

But it adds also:

Parents have a prior right to choose the kind of education that shall be given to their children. (Article 26, 3)

While the Universal Declaration of Human Rights expresses no more than shared ideals, it is important in view of the last limitation to mention also the clause in the positively endorsed International Covenant on Economic, Social and Cultural Rights which, after specifically recognising the responsibility of the family for education, continues:

The States Parties to the present Covenant undertake to have respect for the liberty of parents, and, when applicable, legal guardians to choose for their children schools, other than those established by the public authorities, which conform to such minimum educational standards as may be laid down or approved by the State and to ensure the religious and moral education of their children in conformity with their own convictions.

No part of this article shall be construed so as to interfere with the liberty of individuals and bodies to establish and direct educational institutions. (Article 13, 3 and 4)

Finally, the European Convention for the Protection of Human Rights and Fundamental Freedoms includes the following:

Everyone has the right to respect for his private and family life, his home and his correspondence. (Article 8)

No person shall be denied the right to education. In the exercise of any functions which it assumes in relation to education and to teaching, the State shall respect the right of parents to ensure such education and teaching in conformity with their own religious and philosophical convictions. (Article 2 of Protocol to the Convention)

The distinction between the negative rights asserted initially and the positive rights subsequently claimed in the social, cultural and economic spheres has been remarked upon by a number of commentators. Maurice Cranston argues that economic and social rights, which may even be held to include such improbable (because unrealisable on a world scale) entitlements as a right to holidays with pay cannot logically be considered universal human rights and that the attempt to treat them as such has vitiated the whole enterprise of protecting human rights through such agencies as the United Nations.[9]

He gives three main reasons for this criticism. First, that the rights traditionally claimed are mainly rights against government interference and are easily secured by legislation, while economic and social rights may be either impossible of attainment or at least require a vast government apparatus for their achievement. Secondly, he argues that universal rights must of necessity be rights for all simply by virtue of their human status, but the new class of rights includes categories which are applicable only to certain individuals (for example, in the case of paid holidays, those who are in paid employment). Finally, he argues that universal rights must pass the test of importance - they must not be essentially trivial, as some of the listed economic and social rights become when set against the older claims for the freedom of the human spirit or the right to life itself.

Cranston's interpretation of the swing of Marxist and also Third World opinion away from repudiation of rights, when narrowly and negatively specified as setting limits to the power of government, towards endorsement of a vast battery of economic and social rights is that it legitimises the pursuit of economic progress in preference to, and possibly at the expense of, the freedom of the individual. It has already been argued that Marxist thought devalues the individualism implicit in the negative rights of the Lockean tradition. Whether or not, therefore, Cranston is correct in his analysis of the motivation behind this development, it must be conceded that the Lockean concept needs to be safeguarded against opposition which might attempt to obliterate rather than destroy it, by burying the diamond of freedom in a slag-heap of welfare and economic progress.

The idea that the Lockean view of human rights is best represented as a hard diamond of truth amongst obfuscating additions would not, however, be universally accepted. Melden, for example, regards the negative rights derived from Locke as seriously defective and urges a radical revision of the notion of rights based on revised notions of what it is to be a person. He writes:

> It has become painfully evident that in a complex and highly competitive industrial society much more is required in order to safeguard human rights than measures that protect the interests of the advantaged, measures which succeed only in enabling those favoured by the accidents of birth and fortune to employ their superior abilities and opportunities to improve their estates to the neglect and even at the expense of others. We now recognise, many or most of us at least, that the obligations imposed upon governments, civic groups and individuals, in recognition of the fundamental moral rights of all persons, is [*sic*] to seek to reduce the effects of the natural inequalities among persons, effects which if allowed to go unchecked would deprive many of the rights they have as human beings.[10]

Amongst the factors requiring to be checked by government and other action, Melden cites poverty, lack of education, physical and mental disease, and defects in the system of criminal justice and punishment. It is these problems that generate the welfare rights favoured in contemporary declarations but open to the criticisms put forward by Cranston. Melden's view is persuasive: governments which attack poverty and other ills are the kind of governments which satisfy many human aspirations and open the door to the satisfaction of others. But even in conceding so much it must be recognised that this itself is the localised viewpoint of Western materialist societies, and that other societies are founded on other values, rating, for example, the elimination of poverty as a lower priority than conformity to religious ideals. But it must be questioned whether, in any case, the determination to eliminate social evils should be expressed in terms of rights. Cranston is substantially correct when he says that the essential characteristics of rights are ignored when this is done. The area described by Melden is an area where equality and fraternity are the functioning ideals, while the area of rights is predominantly the area of liberty.

This conflict, however, leaves scope for compromise where education is concerned, for here both positive and negative rights may be accommodated. It has been argued here that there is a right to education at whatever level a society is able to provide out of its resources at a particular time. This is not a right, however, which necessitates or justifies a vast centralised and bureaucratised statewide monopoly of all educational processes. In the last analysis education may be a personal and private enterprise without formal organisation. For this reason, the modern and most recently proclaimed positive right to privacy may well be the right which is of most relevance to education. This is the right which sets the individual in the family context against the individual as an atom in an anonymous and indifferent society. If man has a right to education based on his right to fulfil his deepest nature or to function more fully as a human being, as those like Melden would maintain, urging a revision of human rights on the grounds that negative liberties are not enough, then it is still necessary to guard against the invasion of that deeper personality, that human status, by emphasising the right of individuals to choose the form that education should take.

The right *not* to have a particular kind of education imposed upon an unconsenting family unit is one which the international declarations proclaiming the right to education have, with both foresight (in the light of recent political moves in some liberal democratic countries) and also hindsight (in the light of abuses of the educational process under both fascism and communism), included alongside references to the importance of the individual's cultural development. These declarations enshrine, too, a commitment to the right of individuals to perpetuate their own ideals and beliefs through the family structure by retaining in their own hands ultimate control of the shape and direction of their children's education. Any purely local political moves in a particular country to set aside these restraints must be regarded as serious violations of principles in terms of which the international community has attempted, in however limited or defective a fashion, to identify and give expression to those needs of man which transcend frontiers and national forms of organisation. Against these fundamental considerations, expediency, economic efficiency and social equality are goals which reduce to their correct perspective as, by comparision with liberty, insignificant aspects of the development of the human spirit which is the true goal of education.

NOTES: CHAPTER 9

1   E. Kamenka, 'The anatomy of an idea', in E. Kamenka and A. E.-S. Tay (eds), *Human Rights* (London: Edward Arnold, 1978).
2   F. H. Bradley, *Ethical Studies* (London: Oxford University Press, 1970), pp. 208-9.
3   See, for example, H. L. A. Hart, 'Bentham on legal rights', in A. W. B. Simpson (ed.), *Oxford Essays in Jurisprudence,* 2nd series (London: Oxford University Press, 1973), pp. 171-201.

4   A. I. Melden, *Rights and Persons* (Oxford: Blackwell, 1977), p. 23. See also R. Wasserstrom, 'Rights, human rights and racial discrimination', *Journal of Philosophy,* vol. LXI (1964), pp. 628-41.

5   G. E. Moore, *Principia Ethica* (Cambridge: Cambridge University Press, 1960), ch. 1.

6   J. Kleinig, 'Human rights, legal rights and social change', in E. Kamenka and A. E.-S. Tay (eds), *Human Rights* (London: Edward Arnold, 1978), p. 46.

7   I. Kant, *Lectures on Ethics* (New York: Harper & Row, 1963), p. 194.

8   J. P. Plamenatz, 'Equality of opportunity', in W. T. Blackstone (ed.), *The Concept of Equality* (Minneapolis, Minn.: Burgess, 1969), p. 92.

9   M. Cranston, *What are Human Rights?* (London: Bodley Head, 1973).

10 Melden, op. cit., pp. 244-5.

Bibliography

BOOKS

Archambault, R. D. (ed.) (1965), *Philosophical Analysis and Education* (London: Routledge & Kegan Paul).

Archambault, R. D. (ed.) (1966), *John Dewey on Education, Appraisals* (New York: Random House).

Bantock, G. (1973), *Education in an Industrial Society* (London: Faber).

Barker, R. (1972), *Education and Politics* (London: Oxford University Press).

Barrow, R. (1975), *Moral Philosophy for Education* (London: Allen & Unwin).

Berlin, I. (1970), *Four Essays on Liberty* (London: Oxford University Press).

Blackstone, W. T. (ed.) (1969), *The Concept of Equality* (Minneapolis, Minn.: Burgess).

Boyd, D. (1973), *Elites and their Education* (Slough: NFER).

Bradley, F. H. (1970), *Ethical Studies* (London: Oxford University Press).

Brown, S. C. (ed.) (1975), *Philosophers Discuss Education* (London: Macmillan).

Cornford, F. M. (1955), *The Republic of Plato* (London: Oxford University Press).

Cranston, M. (1973), *What are Human Rights?* (London: Bodley Head).

Crick, B. and Porter, A. (1978), *Political Education and Political Literacy* (London: Longman).

Dancy, J. C. (1963), *The Public Schools and the Future* (London: Faber).

DES (1966), *Children and their Primary Schools,* a report of the Central Advisory Council for Education (London: HMSO).

Dewey, J. (1916), *Democracy and Education* (New York: Macmillan/The Free Press).

Doyle, J. F. (ed.) (1973), *Educational Judgements* (London: Routledge & Kegan Paul).

Duncan, G. (1973), *Marx and Mill* (Cambridge: Cambridge University Press).

Eliot, T. S. (1948), *Notes towards the Definition of Culture* (London: Faber).

Flew, A. (1976), *Sociology, Equality and Education* (London: Macmillan).

Friedman, M. (1962), *Capitalism and Freedom* (Chicago: University of Chicago Press).

Garforth, F. W. (ed.) (1971), *Mill's Educational Writings* (Columbia, NY: Teachers College Press, Columbia University).

Gilkes, A. N. (1957), *Independent Education: in Defence of the Public Schools* (London: Gollancz).

Glennerster, H. (1970), *Paying for Private Schools* (London: Allen Lane).

Hampshire, S. (ed.) (1978), *Public and Private Morality* (Cambridge: Cambridge University Press).

Hayek, F. A. (1968), *The Constitution of Liberty* (London: Routledge & Kegan Paul).

Hayek, F. A. (1976), *Individualism and Economic Order* (London: Routledge & Kegan Paul).

Heater, D. (ed.) (1969), *The Teaching of Politics* (London: Methuen).

Hirsch, F. (1976), *Social Limits to Growth* (London: Routledge & Kegan Paul).

Hirst, P. (1974), *Moral Education in a Secular Society* (London: University of London Press).

Hobhouse, L. T. (1971), *Liberalism* (London: Oxford University Press).

Hollins, T. H. B. (ed.) (1964), *Aims in Education* (Manchester: Manchester University Press).

Hook, S. (1980), *Philosophy and Public Policy* (Carbondale, Ill.: Southern Illinois University Press).

Illich, I. (1971), *De-Schooling Society* (London: Calder & Boyars).

Kalton, G. (1966), *The Public Schools: a Factual Survey* (London: Longman).

Kamenka, E. (1969), *Marxism and Ethics* (London: Macmillan).

Kamenka, E. and Tay, A. E.-S. (eds.) (1978), *Human Rights* (London: Edward Arnold).

Kant, I. (1963), *Lectures on Ethics* (New York: Harper & Row).

Kuhn, T. (1970), *The Structure of Scientific Revolutions* (Chicago: University of Chicago Press).

Kupperman, J. (1970), *Ethical Knowledge* (London: Allen & Unwin).

Lambert, R. and Staff, S. (1968), *New Wine in Old Bottles? Studies in Integration with the Public Schools* (London: Bell).

Langford, G. and O'Connor, D. J. (eds) (1973), *New Essays in Philosophy of Education* (London: Routledge & Kegan Paul).

Lukes, S. (1973), *Individualism* (Oxford: Blackwell).

Manning, D. J. (1976), *Liberalism* (London: Dent).

Marcuse, H. (1969), *An Essay on Liberalism* (Boston, Mass.: Beacon Press).

Marx, K. (1962), *The Poverty of Philosophy* (Moscow: Foreign Languages Publishing House).

Marx, K. (1962), *Selected Works* (Moscow: Foreign Languages Publishing House).

Melden, A. I. (1977), *Rights and Persons* (Oxford: Blackwell).

Mill, J. S. (1954), *On Liberty* (London: Dent, Everyman).

Mill, J. S. (1954), *Utilitarianism* (London: Dent, Everyman).

Mill, J. S. (1954), *Autobiography* (London: Dent, Everyman).

Moore, G. E. (1960), *Principia Ethica* (Cambridge: Cambridge University Press).

Nozick, R. (1974), *Anarchy, State and Utopia* (Oxford: Blackwell).

O'Connor, D. J. (1957), *Introduction to the Philosophy of Education* (London: Routledge & Kegan Paul).

O'Neill, O. and Ruddick, W. (eds) (1979), *Having Children* (Oxford: Oxford University Press).

Peters, R. S. (1966), *Ethics and Education* (London: Allen & Unwin).

Peters, R. S. (ed.) (1967), *The Concept of Education* (London: Routledge & Kegan Paul).

Public Schools Commission (1968), *Report* (London: HMSO).

Raphael, D. D. (ed.) (1967), *Political Theory and the Rights of Man* (London: Macmillan).

Rawls, J. (1972), *A Theory of Justice* (London: Oxford University Press).

Robinson, G. (1971), *Private Schools and Public Policy,* Loughborough Occasional Papers in Economics and Social Research No. 1 (Loughborough: Department of Social Sciences and Economics, Loughborough University of Technology).

Rousseau, J. J. (1966), *Emile* (London: Dent, Everyman).

Rubenstein, D. and Stoneman, C. (eds) (1970), *Education for Democracy* (Harmondsworth: Penguin).

Sargant, W. (1963), *Battle for the Mind* (London: Pan).

Simpson, A. W. B. (ed.) (1973), *Oxford Essays in Jurisprudence,* 2nd series (London: Oxford University Press).

Skillen, A. (1977), *Ruling Illusions* (Hassocks: Harvester Press).

Snook, I. (1972), *Concepts of Indoctrination* (London: Routledge & Kegan Paul).

Snook, I. (1972), *Indoctrination and Education* (London: Routledge & Kegan Paul).

Snook, I. and Lankshear, C. (1979), *Education and Rights* (Melbourne: Melbourne University Press).

Talmon, J. L. (1961), *The Origins of Totalitarian Democracy* (London: Mercury Books).

Tawney, R. H. (1964), *Equality* (London: Allen & Unwin).

Townsend, P. and Bosanquet, N. (1972), *Labour and Inequality* (London: Fabian Society).

Wolff, R. P., Moore, B. and Marcuse, H. (1969), *A Critique of Pure Tolerance* (London: Cape).

Young, M. (ed.) (1971), *Knowledge and Control, New Directions for the Sociology of Education* (London: Collier Macmillan).

ARTICLES

Cohen, B. (1975), 'Principles and situations - the liberal dilemma and moral education', *Proceedings of the Aristotelian Society,* vol. LXXVI.

Cohen, B. (1977), 'Three ethical fallacies', *Mind,* vol. 86.

Kordig, C. R. (1979), 'The rights of conscience', *The New Scholasticism,* vol. 53, pp. 375-87.

Marples, R. (1978), 'Is religious education possible?', *Journal of Philosophy of Education,* vol. 12, pp. 81-91.

Sealey, J. (1979), 'Education as a second-order form of experience and its relation to religion', *Journal of Philosophy of Education,* vol. 13, pp. 83-90.

Smolicz, J. J. (1974), 'The concept of tradition: a humanistic interpretation', *The Australian and New Zealand Journal of Sociology,* vol. 10, no. 2, pp. 75-83.

Smolicz, J. J. (1977), 'The sociology of independent schools', in Proceedings of the National Council of Independent Schools, *New Perspectives in Boarding Schools* (Melbourne: NCIS), pp. 161-90.

Smolicz, J. J. and Secombe, M. J. (1977), 'Cultural interaction in a pluralist society', *Ethnic Studies,* vol. 1, no. 1, pp. 1-15.

Wall, G. (1975), 'Moral authority and moral education', *Journal of Moral Education,* vol. 4, no. 2, pp. 95-9.

Wasserstrom, R. (1964), 'Rights, human rights and racial discrimination', *Journal of Philosophy,* vol. LXI, pp. 628-41.

Index